SUB DIVO

SUB DIVO

NORM SIBUM

POEMS

BIBLIOASIS

FIRST EDITION

Library and Archives Canada Cataloguing in Publication

Sibum, Norm, 1947-
    Sub divo / Norm Sibum.

Poems.
ISBN 978-1-926845-96-8

    I. Title.

PS8587.I228S92 2012   C811'.54   C2012-901707-8

Readied for the Press by Eric Ormsby

  Canada Council for the Arts **Conseil des Arts du Canada** **ONTARIO ARTS COUNCIL** **CONSEIL DES ARTS DE L'ONTARIO** Canadian Heritage Patrimoine canadien

Biblioasis acknowledges the ongoing financial support of the Government of Canada through the Canada Council for the Arts, Canadian Heritage, the Canada Book Fund; and the Government of Ontario through the Ontario Arts Council.

PRINTED AND BOUND IN CANADA

 MIX
Paper from responsible sources
FSC www.fsc.org FSC® C004071

 ANCIENT FOREST ™ FRIENDLY

Contents

Leaving Circe

"You," said Circe to Odysseus come
To do battle with her magic
And retrieve his men from her handiwork
By which she had taken some liberties with human forms,
"Dissembler, you've been expected."

"You," said Circe to a lordly wretch, his heart in his mouth
At the sight of his fellow travellers brought so low,
And yet, here he was stifling his rising laughter,
"I know you're the apple in the eyes of the gods.
But think twice before you think to get the best of me."

A glittering of light in his eyes. She continued:

"Promise you pleasures, give you a break
From the wrack and pain of your mortal lot,
And you fall for the trick: wine and caresses lose you your minds.
And you wonder why women hold men in secret contempt?
Then again, we women, we tire, too,
Of all the ways that you would have us.
What recompense? Sporadic pleasure, a brief interlude
In the toil and pain—Thank Zeus I have a witch's arts—
Such a bore, don't you think, that we meet like this,
Each the hostage of the other?
So you're the intelligent one.
How do you like my menagerie?
How it twitters, whines, gesticulates.
Are you thirsty? Try a cup of this—"

Circe's ploy transparent, Odysseus replied:

"The leaf I just now chewed shall spare my senses
The poison in your honeyed draught.
Your honeyed words? They're nothing to me.
But yes, I've sometimes wondered it: why,
Why spurn the likes of you for death and a mortal wife
Who has all my faults on her mind?
Perhaps because she's all I know, really,
That and the treachery of men and the sea,
You deities extra degrees of difficulty.
My pleasures? They are a swallow of my own vintage,
My cheese, the goodly scent of my wife's armpit.
The sight of my old father, my hunting dog—
Yes, come to think of it, my hunting dog—"

Circe, seeing it was hopeless, said: "Yes. Delightful. How good for you.
There is nothing for it then but to reverse my charm,
And pretty beastliness return to wretchedness,
You and your playmates free to go,
Subject to your destinies—"

And she with a smirk offered up
Famed Odysseus her scented cheek.
He, without ceremony, sniffed and kissed it.
Yes, it would seem he was dismissive,
Waving his *see you around* while showing his men—
Besotted sailors still, blinking in a sudden onrush of light—
The way out of their terrible dream.
Greeks went for their boats.
As if they'd learned something.
As if they ever would.

Frieda Sue Vagolin

She who loved Schumacher the pedagogue
Adored him, too, for what he dreamed
As he'd wander the staircase with his muse
And the death-defying leaps of poesy
The muse was accustomed to
In the clapboard palace on Pleasant Hill.
   This clapboard palace on Pleasant Hill
   Where it overlooked an arm of the sea
   Was true to mist and true to tugs
   And float planes and freighters and mackinaws,
   Was benign of aspect above the lumber mills
   And the sometimes tomb-like, sometimes raucous
                    beer parlours where
   Men with fingers gone drank their beer.
And Frieda Sue Vagolin, a woman of the mist
Such as might hang in the branches of arbutus
And settle on tam and whisky flask, she was true
   To the man who relished the taste of words
   As surely as each day's new sun, if the rain held off,
   Hit the new ground running
   And romped through the window of a room
   And in and around the objects of a room,
   And how it shone on the countenances of love—
   Such sweethearts they were, Frieda Sue and her lover boy,
   Pillow to pillow, nested there—

§

And she knew he was boyishly blasted
When he was come home in ripe tenor,

As if for the express purpose of incantation:
"O Bright Apollo, in your eye-O."
Sometimes they'd manage to make love before
He crashed, before he forgot the name he must whisper—hers,
Before he passed out at the top of the stairs.
He'd say in her ear, he'd insinuate things there
 Of a past in which she had no interest, to be sure,
 About which so many got so much in error—

 "You know, my sweet, my effable Frieda Sue,
 The beginning and the end mirror each other
 Even in what was Old Mother Russia
 That got to be a cautionary tale.
 You see, the Great Man dying, beshat himself,
 Half his brain blown up in the Russian night,
 Which some say was foul play, some natural cause.
 And everything got loose, Beria's brain getting whims:
 Saw himself now as First Deputy Premier,
 The Great Man, not yet dead, not yet all brain-dark,
 And my head, oh, it's going off. Oh, oh and oh. Off—"

And Frieda Sue Vagolin she would rally
Her knees as much as she was able to
And catch all that dread and catch all that love
There at the top of the stairs, her denims slung down
To her rosy calves, he all the way off now that he was spent,
Was once again the cuckold of his passions, he, even so, having figured
 The man was quite the predator, Joseph Vissarionovich Stalin,
 First General Secretary of the Communist Party of the Soviet Union's
 Central Committee, who purged and purged and purged, even his intimates.

 —*Stalin and the poets, Stalin and the generals, the kulaks, the western libs*—

§

Now Schumacher was, among other things, more than a poet,
More than a lover boy, than a pedagogue of some discipline—

This Schumacher, for a portion of each day, every day of the year,
He was a grammarian, he who'd written
A treatise on language's sticky points—
    Pronoun agreements, dangling particips,
    And *that* versus *which* and *its* and *it's*—
And then he'd shut his eyes and images would swim
In that part of his brain where poems have origin,
    And in a poem he could never complete
    Was Hector sweet-talking the wife,
    Hector tickling Astyanax under the chin:
    How a father should comport himself
    Even as the incipient flames of an unholy mess
    Reached for Troy in loving embrace.
    And it was the dream of a poem he was born to write
    That he would always dream and fail to write,
    That he'd think through for hours on end—in the Hotel Carolyn,
    In the beer reek and beer smoke wafting
    To the cracked rafters of the cavern,—
    Implacable life, absurd tenderness
    In the company of old Slavs from the mill,
    In the company of toothless Salish whores,
    Ancient Brits reliving defunct empire,
    His own comrades, pissed and stoned and funked,
    On about *Stalin and the poets, Stalin and the generals, kulaks, the libs,*
    And what happened to those Mayans, anyway?

§

Frieda Sue Vagolin? Grammarian's mistress? She whom some men found
A little light on brains but comely enough,
Who had love everywhere you touched her, but only for a Chosen One?
She worked three days a week for Blundell the lush
And esteemed publisher of books, she his Girl Friday, stellar object of
                                        incompetent lust
The management of which was not her boss's strong point,
He who had discreet recourse to prostitution
Even as he talked up the evils of heroin
And such narcotics as got any dreamer through
The day-to-day blahs of the means of production—
And once in a time that at one time was sacred,
Blundell had a firebrand's regard for merit,
Merit, that is, on the part of poets
And writers of tales and whatnot.
But no, it didn't last, and Frieda Sue Vagolin she
Put up with hands that roved and pirated, even as she pitied the man,
As she couldn't fault those hands, really,
    Her bosom splendid, holy, consecrated,
    Meant for Schumacher the pedagogue
    Who was now and then smitten with it, agog—
But when other men on Sundays played their golf,
Schumacher made the trek to the house of Blundell
There across town, up on the fine mountain, fabulous house
Of cedar planks and marble fixtures and things precious,
    And they'd argue, they'd debate, irritate and one-up
    Each other, drinking like the fishes.

    Blundell, speaking power to truth: "Stalin had it right when he said
    That when it comes to verses of love,
    There ought only be two books, no more—
    One for him and one for her. Conflagrate the rest—"

"Yes," said Schumacher, swilling his Black Russian—disgusting swill,
"For the most part, life is mostly Gunga Din,
And then there are pronouns, difficulties, Stalin."
Stalin and the poets, Stalin and the generals, kulaks, the libs—

§

Oh, everyone had a vision to put on offer,
A vision of what's best for people,
A vision of water, a vision of bread,
Wine for the people, figs for the people
And a flower in every person's lapel—
And though Schumacher was always potted, almost sober he
Talked the logic of power, always and ever power's logic,
To which remarks Blundell only idly blinked
As he was mild of nature on the surface
But could've been top-echelon police
With shadows at his command,

While Frieda Sue Vagolin, amply bestowed
With what ordinary men found entrancing,
Blundell ordinary enough to wonder if he himself was only average,

She marked the hour at a table in the Hotel Carolyn,
In the company of Schumacher's anarchists,
Decrepit Slavs, Salish whores,
And she fretted at the thought of Blundell
Taking another bite of her lover boy's,
Her grammarian's, her poet's fine innocence.

Oh, perhaps you'll find it hard to credit
That a poet would sport on his person

A fine innocence as well as a nose for what's
Really real, inasmuch, when you get down to it,
   And in Blundell's sunken living room they'd get down to it,
   Arguing Stalin, God and Charles Dickens
   And what it is about women that drives men insane
                              and off their game.
   But Schumacher, seeing as he was always potted and almost sober—
   O Bright Apollo, in your eye-O—
   No longer knew with what he trucked,
   Be it God or love or muse or Frieda Sue.
And funny one should mention her, he now fired-up
For the wench.
So then, madcap, Odysseus in a sprint, a dash across town,
He hunkered over the wheel of the coughing Volkswagen,
And now the bridge and now the side streets
So as to avoid the cops out for their DUIs.
(But then, if the beer parlour was open it couldn't be Sunday
And so, which day, which month, which year of Our Lord
Or which of O Bright Apollo, if it came to that?)—
   And into the beer parlour to grab her, effable Frieda Sue,
   And back to the house and then up the stairs
   To paw for a moment's worth of eternity,
   His head lolling with sex and Stalin,
   Her legs wrapped around his blushing neck,
   His thoughts wrapped around vast slaughter
   And the logic of power and the absurdity of sense—
And she was catching dread and love for a rainy day,
Smelling on him the cigarettes he'd smoked that day.
There was the beginning in him of belches—
Pickled eggs from noontime lunches.

§

Schumacher always potted and almost sober,
The god always counselled discretion and patience and a nap
Before nooky pursuant to other comforts,
And he'd fall asleep before he could begin to gush,
To weep for all the dying and rapine in life,
At which Stalin, among others, had been past master,
Before she could shush him and rock him
And mother his silly little insipid heart—

Yes, if she could only hold him tight
And lock in his love and it never die,
This man who left around the house
Notes on which were names, names, and more names
That testified to his curiosity, his intelligence
Or lack thereof,

Like Trofim Lysenko, question mark,
Like Beria and what he was up to when
Stalin's heart went bust—question marks, Khruschev and Zhukov being, no doubt,
Two likely hombres what did Beria the sex hound in—
Prokofiev—*opportunist?*—more question marks—

Or Isaak Babel. Now who was he? Or so Frieda Sue Vagolin
Would think it through—if only she had a clue,
Come across yet more notes in her palace of a house
Up on Pleasant Hill overlooking a paradise of sorts,
And she read Schumacher's scribbled answer to himself:

'Babel—writer—knew bunches of
Cabbies and whores, knew layabouts, cutthroats, thieves,
Shabby poets, done in by Stalin—1940, was it?

Prokofiev the Richard Strauss of the Stalin realm,
Just that maybe, maybe he was dispirited *by all that realm*—'

§

And she, uncomplicated woman,
One who was free, for the most part, of undue expectation,
Just that a girl should be adored,

She came to miss her Schumacher most
When she was in the shower, pleasuring
In the stinging jet rays of pentecostal water,
Drawing the blood to the surface of her skin,

And he was not right there to marvel, peeking in,
And then to instruct her in a matter of history,
Observing that Prokofiev died one day after Stalin
But had to settle for paper flowers at his funeral
As all the real blooms for miles around were bespoke,
Reserved for the Great Man's death debauch—

§

And it was almost subversive and endearing how
Blundell the publisher got it into his head
To defraud the government of some monies
By one misbegotten scam or other—his kind of book rated it,

While at the college where pedagogues worked their mills,
There came to be a craze for gender-neutral filler—
Like pronouns, for instance, the fact of which
Cut Schumacher the grammarian to the quick,

The poet, the lover boy, the fine fellow in him
Otherwise all for rights, rights of property or otherwise,
And whatever the darlings wanted, be it proper paycheques,
Be it civilized vacations on the Costa del Sol,
Or the presidency, or rooms of their own,
Or brunches with real-life princesses,—

But he was troubled, no denying that, disturbed
By what it was that was coming unglued
In the language, in a currency of exchange
That was so much more than just protocol,
So much so the notes now flew around the house
That sat on the summit of Pleasant Hill
And caught the breezes there,—
    That said that Stalin held his darlings in no great regard,
    Were herrings with ideas, though Stalin raped them, anyway,
    And then disappeared their husbands, liking his wine sweet,
    His tobacco strong, liking his Tarzan films,
    Would've thought Frieda Sue a cow,
    A delectable specimen, no doubt, but a cow—
And, too bad, but Frieda Sue saw,
With her own eyes, the gist of the scribblings.

A dispassionate remark or a scurrilous bit of umbrage?—
So Frieda Sue, stung,
Wondered as she read her lover boy's scrambled thinking—

§

And she saw the light over a period of months
Go out of the eyes of her estranged sweetheart,
As if he were in a once familiar world become strange to him,

The cruelties of Stalin less peculiar than
    The politics of language in bed with market forces,
    The logic of power, always and ever the logic of power
    Explaining the insufferably unsexed pronouns
    Of a counter-reformation, nothing noble in them.
    Then the half-hearted f—king. Then the death in her poet of poetry.
    Or that lover boy thought it pointless to 'muse-ify'.
    Even more pointless to encourage Blundell in his ruses
    That were, at any rate, nothing more than drunken ruses
    Born of an evening's want of amusement,
    Testifying to a cynic's loss of faith—

§

In any case, Frieda Sue Vagolin (and there was
Love in her teeth and heart and fingertips
And toe and spleen and the gorgeous mole
On the underswell of her left breast,
And in the vast arenas of her eye-O's),
Reduced to all her worst fears and then some,
They found Schumacher's body in the course of time,
Found it on Virgin's Island where he used to sun himself,
    The island all rock and snakes, his head exploded,
    Found it in the wettest drizzle in the world,
    Found it there with his grammar book, the one he wrote,
    Its *its* and *it's* underscored, pronouns arrowed through.

And Frieda Sue Vagolin perhaps knew now
How it is the logic of power drives people mad,
How it was that Stalin drove men and women mad,
And she no longer wondered at Schumacher's childlike scrawl

Even if she never got over it, his going off,
Holding the pieces of her heart together between her fists.

And no, she never got weary of the rage
   That would come on her and steal her show of peace,
   Especially after the college's squalid show of grief,
   And Blundell's sidling up to her to milk her grief
   And twit the soul of chivalry—

And she came to know that it's a mistake
To stop and explain oneself, and yet,
How simple an explanation it was she had in mind:

   That days come about unexpected, unlooked-for, fine days they are
   Of life until it's death—
   Staff meetings all raid and counter-raid,
   And everyone's a brute, man or woman,
   And everyone claims fealty, man or woman,
   And everyone's a poet and pedagogue, man or woman,
   And a lover boy and a grammarian, man or woman.

   But as it was with the heart she loved,
   And if only she knew if it had loved her back,
   It must've gotten to be such a dry little stick—
   Silly insipid little heart snapped in two.

Prometheus on the Terrasse

What pecks at my liver, so to speak,
With such assiduous enthusiasm,
And that she who lives above the garden shop
Inflames me with her average thoughts,
Is the farce there is in all we do,
And the sorrow within, in all we do,
The history of our histories tumbling on
Like an angel looking for its God.

Or that Chronos—another mark—
He sticks his well-etched mug
Deep in a pot of gassy sweet stuff
From which honey the Eternal goes
And crawls into his gypsum eyes
So much so, he now dreams
Forever, perhaps, of girls and such
Who live above garden shops
Of shears and rakes and seed and fertilizer.
—It'll rain, this afternoon, a balmy, planting rain
    Of hammering cloud Greeks never knew,
    Our best aspirations for our double-dealing kind
    A little matter of our true minds,
    And we, like some king of an ancient past,
    Would address flowers in swampy ditches, and blind,
    Coolly stare down the setting sun.

It was not the gift of fire yours truly wasted
When I gave it all away
To Cyr and Labrosse and Robertson
That raised the hackles of an investigatory committee,—

No, it was the fire in my heart the gods found suspect
For its being but nominal passion
As when a girl who lives above a garden shop,
Bored to tears, does her nails—
—Hot rain. A rain to wash the deepening green of leaves
      And splash the impetuous snub noses of
      Lovers who love for the self-help of loving,
      Sunday funnies cruising for their laughs—

May, and foliage thickens here.
And religion and science fatten here
On the leavings of unforgiving atmospheres.
Otherwise, the neighbourhood smacks
Of pistils of sacred Louisiana sauce.
What's up with those darlings there in their café chairs?
Why, there's never been the like: white-hot egos,
Secular smooches Roman to the core.

And some speak moral aesthetics in the quaintest of places
Where the vines have been pruned for a thousand years.
Oh just pass the soda water. Give that demiurge his saltine, will you,
Lest the hunger in his eyes kills ours.
It's going to take another end of empire
Before the populace even begins to get it:
How, for each their giddiness of self, they're despised—
Or moral force that has purchase but is short on traction
Would apologize to a world in which power's the thing.
Let the conquistador say he civilized brutes
From one end of Peru to the ends of the earth,
You'll hear laughter in all the waiting rooms
Of all the imperial paradises, even in Gaza, law's rule
Convenient now except when it isn't—

Look, I who kissed her laughing lips more than once
Only to inflame all over again
The gnostic fires in my belly,
Saw that nothing explains a thing—

Look, to hear some tell it, all we need is mind
And we'll break through the old conundrum
That has been our lot since the gods punted
And chained me here with invisible links,
With winks and nods and citations galore.
And though I get about, and yes, I do get about
With my mind, with extra-virgin sangfroid and a metro pass,
Though I carry a semi-warm torch
For one who lives above a garden shop
And weighs as much as any whim weighs—or next to nothing,—
Though I've pleasant girth around my waist
From the pastas I've swallowed down, I say that some people, God bless them,
They're an optimistic breed that can never accept
The best thinking has gone for naught—

And the girl who lives above a garden shop
And has sweaty sex with her idle loves,
She who, by the flickering flames of nine white candles,
Reads the *Metamorphoses* and wears men's shirts,—
She who remains a distant figure on my horizon,—
This sylph who lives above a garden shop
With its seed and pruners, with its top of the line tree branch-trimmers,
With its toxins that treat with voluminous lawns,
She's a diffident muse who mostly shrugs,
She tumbling into a future from a diffident now,
This bland Panthea who either lures men on
Or eludes their grasp. For if men were part gods, is she not all devil still,

She crass and mostly genial
Who sees something coming for which she'll not be blamed,
This unlikely finisher of a marathon,
Her hygiene, however, open to question?
And the gulf breeze that has come like Oedipus
To this cold terrasse, that flowers in and out of the senses
Like love will swell, like hate with all its reasons,
Is alien to her soul and yet, my, but look,
Look how she thrives on it,
Smiling teeth aglow with it,
Her mug bloody from the kill
On which she forever feasts—

And what pecks at my liver, so to speak,
With such assiduous enthusiasm,
And that she who lives above the garden shop
Inflames me with her average thoughts,
Is the farce there is in all we do,
And the sorrow within, in all we do,
The history of our histories tumbling on
Like an angel looking for its God—

Concert by the River, or, Apocryphal Voices

Programme:
Elgar – *Enigma Variations*
Prokofiev – *Romeo and Juliet* (selections)
Sibelius – the Second Symphony

—for MK

I

Is there a statute that stipulates
A man must amuse a woman
While on municipal property,
Moon on the rise?

Well, are you one to point
A finger at the mayor
And point out the sights?
Are you one to whistle
Your admiration of a sky,
The gulls in the haze orchestral?

That their cries amplify your inwardness.
That the night will be hot and sweet.
That you are just now with Morrisette.
That her arms are bare to a whiff of breeze.

Smarter, more learned women than she
Have been, how shall we say, charmed
By your non sequiturs, yes, such as these:

Shall we bring on Debussy, born 1862?
Triangulate a postmodernist to a monkey in the zoo?
Why, Orlando, are you always fooling?

Fill your eyes with the river vista.
With the high bridge from which the lonely
Leap—

II

Soft beneath your thin skin of lust, almost tender toward the lass,
You're not fooling now: you'd hold her hand but for the heat.
And you'd walk her toward the setting sun
Though the river obstructs your feet.

Oh, had you a true grasp of
Matters of philosophy, you'd avow
That Locke was Bob to Kant's crooning Bing,
And fate and destiny aren't the same fish.
But what's that to your companion who lifts
Her modest dress to air her legs
And tell you of what the instant is made?

III

Gulls wheel and swoop—sibilant leaves
Divide the breeze. "Time is motion," so the river insists.
"The mind is no machine," you say, unsure that it's not.
So many gaps in your science.
So much in your heart is God's discarded abyss.
What a lovely sound, though, those boat engines chugging.

The chill waterway, too, calls to your doubt
That man and nature are one,
A mutual idyll, even—

But of women whose dull voices dull
The more they are bitter, out of countenance
Because they've been bullied by husbands

Or because they've none to stiff?
Time to let her know that, at love, you're hopeless.
"Hopeless, hopeless. Really."
(But see, she'll not pity you this.)
Instead, here's what she enthuses:
"Must God love what He made?
When will the music start?
Who said love is born in pain?
I wish we had some gum."

IV

Rose-light, to the west, near empyrean, apes
The highest union with the highest bliss.
In it, an airplane gains altitude.
The orchestra tunes.

And yet, the senses deceive, and kisses being kisses, one such kiss
Could trigger the alarm, could advise the heart
That *this is false.*

In which case the light of day withdraws.
In which case a dog sniffs the grass.
In which case the brain calculates what the nerves relay.

And men are men and women are women, as it was said
In more romantic days, *the friends pictured within—*

V

But some who esteem love do not, in fact, cherish.
That Olivia Proud broke you on her bed.
That she tossed what remained of you
To her boon companions.

That she fed you peppers stuffed with cheese.
Thought she was interested—

Yes, the moon could fall and conflicts ripen.
The music's unanswered enigma just might be
Auld Lang Syne. The moon might slip away and
Another conundrum go,
Go to a grave unsolved.
Surely in this heat the band members melt, Morrisette
Inspecting some split end of hair—

"It must be a hard thing to do – to perform when
The air's this sodden, winds limp, strings gelatinous—"

But no, she'll not laugh, not ever—

Can one hear the silence of a star?
Hear it better if the heart's pure?
Not if you'll think to part her knees.
Should you then write your parliament?
Take up explosives? Then to the streets?

VI

You say, "I'll tell you about my friend Mack the scholar.
Here was a variety of men rolled into one.
Here's Mack boisterous on Olivia's lawn.
He cradles her foot—he sucks her toe.
He's spawn of Pan the mischief-maker—"

But who were those men in rouge who had such airs?
Those cooing women, breasts high and bare?
Who were they who'd been the first to fail?

Their trials of truth: the politics of change, love, literature.
Ah, the famous choreography of a ballet.
Ah, the Nazis or the knights or the dears—

But you were saying—
You forget now—you were saying—

VII

But for the heat, you, Orlando, you'd have at Morrisette.
For time has slowed for the chance, birds massed
For a final go-round in the amorphous sky.

The river grey, smooth, primeval, the city behind you is as spectral
A thing as love.

So you imagine, imagining much,
Including the scherzando ceremony that is out of
Act 1, Scene 2, *Romeo and Juliet*, pertinacious ballet—

"She'd bring us peaches sliced like crescent moons.
She collected men, you know, like they were so many pebbles.
She was a kind of genius in her way."
But Morrisette pranks: "You do seem proud
To have been taken by Olivia Proud."

Even so, on her lips—not even the ghost of a smile—

VIII

Perhaps seduced by the promise of music,
Clouds that built up elsewhere now approach.
Clouds in the shapes of bearded Assyrians—

Is not Morrisette special? Who can hear a woman and think to know her?
Pretty but for the scars that are half her body.
That anger in her eyes—it smoulders.
Does she carry antidotes?
Was Sibelius bilious?

And those parties Olivia threw—you don't know of what they were made.
Great hearts and small hearts took to wine.
Raillery was a kind of silence in a world of lies.

IX
"Well, it was like this," you hear yourself say,
"Girls bestrewed themselves on the grass.
One of them wrote me a Valentine
Only to drop me when I declared my love.

The shadows deepening in the foliage
Seemed to burrow back to distant times.
Whidby wore white, Louise hot pink.
The poet shilled for ultramarine—asked what o'clock it was.
What brings life its unity? What? What propels it towards
Its precipice and fall? Anything at all?"

But Morrisette doesn't know.
Why ever did you think she'd know?
She asks, instead, for a stick of gum.
Gum? You haven't gum—

X
You say, "Scropes had a revelation, Scropes even so, so slow.
He said, 'The new world order is out to do us ill.'

Well, Mack, he smiled his scholar's response of his,
His the smile in which a thousand world orders go to die.
To despise the new world order in full one must
Learn to loathe its critics, and live to tell the tale."
Morrisette leaning closer now—will her eyes crinkle
And she laugh?

XI

And a moon in the haze over the far-off hills—
But can a heron see to fly in darkness?
Must every line of verse
Be absolutely to the point?
For all the heat, is not the woman's wrist cool to the touch,
Black eyes glistening with indecent reserves
Of passionate conviction, of hilarity *now*,—
Of the suspicion that if love runs true,
It mocks itself, is devious to all,
More life footloose in her at just this moment
Than in the river, the grass, the cindery cloud—

XII

So while the darkness is sheathing the intricate
Traceries of the crowns of maples and
The high façades of tall buildings and
The sympathies scored on her countenance,—
While you say, "Mack, for all his insolence,
Was a right good man—lonely—serious,"
Morrisette, restless, bows her head.
She does not believe what tells untruths.
My, what laughter comes out of her—
Night, at last. Night glows in the west.
Mack the turncoat, on a talk show, spoke of

Pre-emption, and,
The eastern sky did get
Its flaming awe.

XIII

What's Mack to her? What Olivia Proud?
Whidby? Louise? Scropes who was incontinent,
So much so he always smelled his fingers?
What you, you and your lugubrious pride?

It's a miracle she lives, body fire-blighted.
Her parent's last drunken sleep.
The world's casual concern.
The world's simpering unconcern
As it is in nature when
The eagle's talons sink in and grasp—
Half her face a stone piazza,
Half her spirit combat-weary—

A buffoon asks (because a buffoon always will):
"When do men get courage? What do
Dragonflies eat? Will the river surge forever and you talk as long?"
Does the computer make me smarter?"

Everyone went to those parties. So much fun.
Whidby wore white, Louise hot pink.
Guess who the poets were? Virulent rainbows of intellect.
And how sweet that river, swift yet meditative.
The clients, to be sure, wore their hearts
And aching kidneys on their sleeves—
Morrisette would hear the Elgar again,
The Elgar that's come and gone. Offer her a cigarette?

Could it be the opening for which she's looked
So as to cup your hand in her cool clutch?
Perhaps. And this is why, you fool,
The night ripening into night and else:
Radical gambits and wars without end,
That something matters more than regard,
The carnage brought on, the disasters sparked
As stone strikes stone, eyes fumbling for love.

Everything and Nothing: The Argument

I

Listen: all is everything. It's nothing, too:
What signifies to me may signify so much less to you.
A thought for paradise or a smaller heaven
Might occupy the mind of a sullen nation
Were it mindful, the August sun spilling light
Between cumular columns in the sky.

II

Now howling dogs, neglected in rooms,
Tell the world that slaves, the dears,
Make the worst of masters
Once they are free to accumulate
Everything, anything and nothing,
The August sun spilling light
Through the windows of a million cubicles.

III

Yes, the August sun spills its largesse
That drifts, because it must, against
Thinking brows and pearly, mindless cloud,
Souls suffering in dreams, souls walking through doors
With love they don't have, with joy they lack,
With pain, if they're old, and regretting much—

IV

And yet old Mrs Orlow happily grinds her jewels
In her shop of stones and baubles
Where biddies and male fuss-budgets meet
And complain of things.

V

And she's always grinning, this unsorrowing
Ancient imp who knows God's bent – *that one can't know it* –
And that dogs will mew when unimpressed
With the more liberal of your liberal intentions.
I spit on your fine poems.

VI

And old Holmes, her red lips sanguine,
Prices her stock of used cassettes –
Creepy musicals and creepy flicks –
There in her emporium of paperbacks
Where biddies and male fuss-budgets meet
And complain of sicknesses.

VII

Beneath which spilling of the light
I reach deep in my sack of what I have for you: *and I spit on the best*
Of your best theories of
Mugabe madness and cougar love
And all the rest—

VIII

Now did you know (Holmes hadn't a clue)
That Tacitus, son-in-law of Agricola who ministered Britain,
Went hard on Tiberius Caesar, withered goat
Who knubbled the private parts of pubescents?
Tiberius Caesar, competent, murderous and burned out,
Cried muddy tears for lost ideals
When he figured no one noticed—
No, can't say I knew or noticed.

But you want a deal? I got 'A Touch So Wicked' and
'Lady in Green and Minor Discretions'
I can let you have at discount—

IX
Beneath which spilling of the light, Leduc, white-haired
And toothless in Quebec, all jammed up in his joints,
Man of the street, consummate romantic,
Roams the street in search of glass,
Plastic, aluminum and honest men
And so, the man turns satanic mills
Into his cost-benefit.

X
Just that we had him to table, last night.
And he who had us in stitches, laughed,
Had earlier come upon, minding *his own business, mind you,*
Strange lusts at the rear of the funeral parlour, *merde,*
Suits going at it, and in this heat—

XI
With love one doesn't have, with joy one lacks—

XII
In light of which Sophie said, 'Cool', and Abigail,
The famous ungainly Abigail, needing always to be
In the best of fits with bosom pals, at the exact centre of regard,
Ears flushed pink at mention of sex,
Rattled the locks of her chaste favours
As if they were so many come-hither
Castanets.

XIII

Beneath which spilling of the light
I stick out my foot and trip your fine poems
That, in all modesty, like Cleopatra's barge,
Would wend their way up the Broad Nile of Life
To Legendary Status.

XIV

Now did you know that Tacitus who wrote the deluxe
Treatment of Rome's imperial highlights – as when Nero aced his mum
Or that he killed her mortally dead
And thought to have a go at her mortified corpse –
Came to see we're rot and filth.
Appetites obscure the will of the gods,
Lovely, death-defying appetites.
The worst of those hungers is 'clarity of mind'.

XV

Sophie, however, launches into *Harry Potter*
That is her sense and sensibility
When she's not depressed—

XVI

And she, anxious, shallow and deep,
As playful as a pup when not depressed,
Looks for love first, and if love is wanting, will
Settle for sensibility, no sense to be had—

XVII

But as for Abigail, kindly and snobbish,
She mustn't, she won't and so, she'll sniff
At thoughts of sin and peccadillo,

But even Scarborough, Toronto, Ontario
Is so much old hat, *so much been there done that*—

XVIII

And yet, make mention of—careful now—the political,
And of a sudden, the lass, she's burbling at the moon
Baying down at her. She knows how infamous
It all is, her famous golden eyes become bronze again
Because, like any throwback, she'd hear more
Lubricious details:
"Oh, do tell more. Don't spare me.
The Congressional Record—my, how fab—"

XIX

And Sophie and Abigail, part party girls, part choristers of doom
That one might easily enough dream into being
As they cluck cool tongues that lick hot sorbets
On the Via Dolorosa—"Poor guy—
They aren't Fabergé, those thorns"—
At any rate, these girls commandeer the lust
Of all the Beccos of the world,
Nominal anti-fascists each of them—

XX

Beneath which spilling of the light
I spit on your fine poems.
Can you imagine—post-textual as reverie? Are there pills?

XXI

Meanwhile, a social-democratic scribe,
There in the *Show Me* state where
The taste of persimmons once puckered my eyes,

With dark guffaws, remarked that, back then,
A reckless and piously psychotic
Political party was willing
To take down the Union in the cause
Of its own provincial interests
(Just that the action applies now, and *in a brand new game*
Of antebellum American roulette)—

XXII

And the far-seer, having remarked thus,
Took himself to the nearest gasthaus
For a riesling, for schnitzel and spaetzl and else,
What with the taste of ruin puckering his
Intestines, *St Louis on the Tiber, the Tiber gaining*
On the Missouri—

XXIII

Beneath which spilling of the light
An early morning thunderstorm
(As if lightning in a jar) produced a name but few details
In my half awake mind: *Gratianus*. Ah yes, he was the last Roman
To cross the Rhine in battle chase. And then he went indolent, knuckling under
Ambrose who reaped the ruin, inimical to Zeus,
But no matter—

XXIV

For here at home, higher powers,
The bank officers Jack and Jill at lunch,
(Born-again, they cancel heaven),
Know that, if time permits, they'll fornicate
And then foreclose—

XXV

A better argument: that Mrs Orlow hears out Puccini
Every third Sunday of the month
Which also happens to be
Her Sunday for red cabbage and pot roast,—
And then a little fruit with a little cream,—
And, bourgeois wind in my sails,
I spit on your fine poems
With my garrulity—

XXVI

Further argument: That who knows how the senate will vote.
Bean counters know how the senate will vote,
And so, the bean counters count, and a petit-bourgeois wind, meanwhile,
Caresses a little the foliage-ample maple boughs
And the light as air fabric with which
Abigail staunches the knock-on effect
Of her famous bosom. But didn't I know,
Surely I must've known that the very same men
Who impeached the president for his trysts
Were, on the sly, diddling their trophy sluts?

XXVII

As for that hole in the dome of Hadrian's Pantheon –
The ocular, jocular, ocularity
Such as lets the August sun spill light,
Through which the sky sometimes pisses
On the foot-worn marble that now and then refracts
The thunder, the lightning, the rain –
It used to impart to emperors godhead,
But to us travellers on the cheap
The buzz of it all.

XXVIII

Went up to a woman in the park.
She, under leafy boughs of shade,
Was selling extraneous household bits
And some hag-celebrity's 'meem-wars'.
And she said, and she was the muse:
"Can't vend to the likes of you,
You patrician of the last principate,
Your feet made not of clay but of snits—"

XXIX

The nation-state redundant, corporate ways the thing,
Corporate wags on *Charlie Rose* joke:
How easy it was to pillage and rape,
And all one required was a little insight
And a little stomach with which to gut
Ohio, the August sun spilling light
Between cumular columns in the sky,
Born-agains praying at a fab god,
Catholics praying to a Catholic god,
And the rest of us to various and sundry gods—

XXX

Yes, and one hears Mexican love songs at 'bratwurst' where
Persians eat aubergine and brain and chilies,
The August sun spilling light
Between cumular columns in the sky,
And one considers that men can cluck,
Arguing flight schedules and the workings of
The Treasury, not to mention Abigail and her
Sweet tooth for insider trading.
Just that men squawk louder than they cluck

When it comes to what truth
Is truly on the money—

XXXI

But then, strike a techno-beat and a leftover god,
Heavy-lifter, still, comes around
In silk and leather, with retrofitting
Lorgnette,

XXXII

Says this Mr Zeus to Miss Mam'selle: "Abigail, good golly, girl,
Yours is the chin of the west's wicked witch.
How it poses. How it pouts. Why, it pirouettes.
Would score points for celibate filth
As would supravene the human legislature.
From its thoughts of filthy virtue,
The once great promise of democracy
Tyrants with cellphones,
Wonks without class.
I spit on your fine poems"—

XXXIII

Under which spilling of the August light
Old Orlow and the Holmes woman see
To things, see to business, keep dead marriages
Alive, as their husbands are dead and buried
But not necessarily lamented.

XXXIV

Whereas Sophie in bathrobe, drying an ear
With a finger poked in a towel,
Understands that when the cops come for her,

It will be for reasons that have to do
With what was *au courant* before
She was even born to this world—

XXXV

And though an amateur of the word once counselled against
The word *indeed* (use of which makes one out a ponce),
I no longer register results with critics.
But to invoke Eros and Thanatos in a single breath
Is to suspire, like they say, on sex and death,
The two ever in a state of *au pair*
In the higher registers of bliss
When one not only discerns the rainbow gases
Of Venus, Bacchus and other mischief, one picks out
A certain silence in one's ears: the infinite.
Yes, indeed.

XXXVI

And everything is all and nothing is all
To you, perhaps, and most likely, to me,
Just that, in light of everything and nothing and all
Their import, signification, crux,
There is always the late lamented embarrassment of sex,
The laughing, the crying, the howling, the messing up,
And the gossip of demise.

Sub Divo

After 69 C.E.

—The empire no longer the plaything of the Julio-Claudians,
his eyes on the future health of the state and its finances, the
unpopular Galba adopted Piso Licianus—

And Galba was murdered, hacked to bits.
And Piso was hauled out of sanctuary, finished off.
The empire proceeded on its merry way.
Mayhem presided, the odd moment of decency.
And then men like us, civil, inoffensive skeptics,
Bottom's up, and to your health, old sport,
Over the course of a few corrosive centuries,
Drank our wine like it was so much sunset
Verse, and one by one, faded from the picture.

Comrades in Arms

Shall we, Eric, rate the chances
 Of the platypus and the cuttlefish?
 What odds, their survival on this earth?

How about your loopy aunts,
 The unconscious cruelties of their dottiness
 Made concrete in moon-bathed cellars, you
  The spiritual heir of *Arsenic and Old Lace?*

But perhaps you've wearied of such pokes at your person,
 The kind that invite farce into the sitting parlour,
 That parts the working man from his union,

That elevates the thinking man with his Rilke
To the Board of Directors and
      Terrible beauties are spewed.

Otherwise, I hardly know where to begin,
 My attempts to write something fine unmanned
By lack of conviction, as if I, too, were born
A stand-up comic, laugh lines my shovel and pick,
And it's not so much a ditch that's dug but ruin.

You, I suppose, see the myriad poisons
 As beautiful, as austere in their pristinities
As those gardens of marble, fig and moon
      In which Caesar's daughter showed some leg.

(Your spell in purgatory will be long, I fear,
      All that classical baggage to freight—)

In the meantime, your pension's busted:
 You're having to work past prime,
The banks, the power brokers playing
All ends against the middle, our old alma mater the U.S.A. squeezed,
Never mind you're squirrelled away in London town,
Poet, scholar, bon vivant, and you mutter a lot,
      And life's fuss and bother, and then you die.

Still, much is permitted, and it's go, go, go, and go some more,
 So that a suburban muse, right-wing diva-lass,
Be she empowered or plain old wife,
Wears a pale peignoir with such flair

That she's a priestess, martini tumblers
    Sacred to her, the swimming pool Avernus.

     —You wouldn't mind a rumble with this dish.
    No more liberal babes for whom poetry is just
One career option among others, the birds flying over flying dead—

And all those Gatsbys bloated with ironies—
Those mobsters, senators, go-betweens
Of the American way of literary greatness? They just keep rubbing
Their golden toilets, their golden parachutes
    To sufficient lustres—

Where does this leave you and I?
Sometimes in restive sleep I've seen us
 Dodging bullets hard by Antietam Creek,
 Heaven and hell but regional offices for a vast consortium—

But to give you a rest, and God knows you need one,
 Is there anyone else around whom I might mug,
 Someone as worthy as you of cheap platitudes,
 Pro forma regrets, some comic put-up job? No?
And all that despair in so many lovely girls,
 All that sweet funk of theirs going to waste—

Whirling Dervishes

I recommend nothing and you recommend less,
Just that we might make of our toes whirling dervishes
If we're pressed, and honour the serapeum like so,
As did the fathers of our fathers,

As will the children of our children,
Human to be born into human rigmarole.

Still, what indolent souls we are,
Presidential in our ideals, Caesars otherwise,
Sleek pashas of cushions, of deep, ruby clarets,
Patriots to nothing more than states of mind.
"Faith," you say, even so.

So faith then, and by faith you would maintain
As when Theophilus barked. Man, did he bark, and down crashed
The exotic deities—rats swarmed out of those hollow spaces,
As a thick dust was raised, and the sky fell
On a faith superceded, the wretches of which cowered a while
And then snapped to, to a new round of imperatives.
Event horizon!

(In light of which both God and Newton's apple have had
Their innings,—and even that science which explains it all,
Our natures, too, even as it drags us by our scruffs
            to the unsullied promise of the stars,
                    will know obsolescence
            by the time we've booked bed and breakfast
                on Saturn's Enceladus, which is a moon.)

Yet, what's with our noses that still we sniff
Messalina's musk, and the bones of imposters that have slept
The sleep of martyrs in cold crypts, the incense, the smoke and mirrors of
Byzantine salons, not to mention the stainless steel excellence
Of our modern mentations, as we were enlightened once,
                and perhaps we recall the signal occasions:
            how we doodled phyllophaga bugs, beetles to you,

in our notebooks, and indulged other acts
Of direct observation? For we know, so much so,
we may believe we know
That every unmade error, every blown superstition of pedigree
May easily enough lead to yet more horrors, more abattoirs
for that flesh somewhere
That always inhabits mistaken spirit.

Eric, this thinking precludes
Plucking grapes at leisure from lustrous bowls,
Is too arduous a business for lying about
On gilded couches, for the breeze-wafted attars
Of the marbled chamber, for glinty and ironic eyes, for all the true sympathies,
And it only bores the darlings who prefer to unassailable truth
diversions that pass the time pleasantly
as well they should.

But here I stall out. I leave to you what thoughts
May bulk up behind that capacious brow of yours,
Should I manage to find you ready, willing and able,
Not somnolent and loathe to do more than wave
At a forest of shadows that we ourselves spawned,
Creeping toward us with its commentary.

Brot und Wein

Eric, you rhymester, heavy-lifter of mind,
As I innocently enough passed by the *Azar*
In a hot breeze, as I considered dining there some evening,
Packing wine to the place, two old biddies on its terrasse,
Each one of those ephemeral dears a hand-painted photograph
Of some cruel but delicate era, spun my head with the perfume

They wore.
They brought me anchorites, brought Theodaras
And the God-crazed, sex-crazed, horse-crazed crowds
Of a capital, and I blinked and I trembled:
       As easy as this to walk along unhinged.

Eric, you outsized cherub, and you may as well have been
The accidental love child
Of a flapper and a Heideggerian,
You tipsy before you even slipped your momma's womb
On being and time, on *Dasein*, as it were, on hereness
And thereness, and God knows what—the Charleston
                    and petting parties?—for once
I myself, most worldly creature, had compassion for
Those men and women who'd trundle off
To live on bugs and sleep in caves and roam
       The heavens and hells of fevered dreams.
And why not? What dream, though it be bizarre fruit,
Denies a dreamer his hothouse redeemer?
           Brot und Wein? Ja oder nein?

You waggler, Eric, of finger and toe, you couch-rider
And contemplative, what with your inner cave art, your Chauvet cinema—
Those charcoal horses, the half-woman half-buffalo god—
Perhaps you, too, harbour a soft heart
For the fools who would extricate
Their madness from a world berserk,
For no other reason than to spite
The ruling class, to twit the middle class (what's left of it)
For its torpors and hysterias, to snub the underbelly
For the vulgarities of vulgar time it craves too much,

Yes, as if religion had anything to do with non-compliance
    Or some values quest on a spiritual plane.

But then, stage spectacle, and here's Theodara, legs spread,
    And here are geese pecking at her privates,
    And she's quite the complicated entity: actress, empress, feminist,
    Woman of God, pornographer, and it's her persuasion
        That brings extinction to an army of rebels in the hippodrome.

And we're right there, aren't we, you love-thief,
    You acolyte of Venus, foot soldier of Hypnos –
    We're there getting our fill of spectacle, rubbing shoulders
        With butcher, baker and candlestick-maker.

And because everyone loves parades and carnivals and fancies
    And such, we remark on the scene and we wonder how long
                            (suspect intellectuals that we are)
    Before we're rounded up, eyes hot-pokered out,
        And slapped into chains for the rest of our lives?
In other words, we haven't the stomach for the solitudes
    Of hermits, and yet, we can't pretend it's anything other than a peep show—
        Rule and being ruled, we poets addicted to the world.

Our True Temper

The annunciating angel asleep at the switch,
You pencilled in for another age, some other heist,
I say to you we change and we stand as we are,
    Ever the same, dauntless circus idiots,
    Ever the light-on-our-feet Fred Astaires of
Creamy, moonlit waltzes the wives adore
        When life goes swimmingly.

So then we crooners of sweet nothings and sundry goods—
Pensive products of pensive mind, jagged thrusts of heart
Such as swell fictions like fermenting fruit
Will swell a crock—we prepare our coffins, and,
As we know ourselves as perishable items,
Or as we resist and hold fast, we cherish
      The battles and hate the wars.

One takes stock, one comprehends
 One has laboured and one has thought
      And who cares? That Carnegie Hall sleight-of-hand?
Better to bellow at frogs in April rain and convince a pond
     Than suffer praise hymns for all the wrong reasons.

Nonetheless, you Golden Child, you mature delinquent
Waggling gnarled-up fingers and toes, you fashion plate
Of gaudy bow ties, star-spangled cummerbunds,
In your dreams you not only go humbly barefoot
To the White House, you kick back in a trailer park
      Such as bivouacs petty need. Yes, why do more when less is more
      In affairs of randiness and making rhymes? And yet,

You'll careen, because bored, at lightspeed through
Cause and effect and the ideas that have had us
By the short hairs—Better to lie about drunk, yes, sheepish and damned
Than to chair a department or change human nature.
No, need for you to gainsay this, sir,
Spiritual inanition our true temper.

And The Dead Move On

Comrade, you're a patriot
Of a country that no longer exists
Save at barbecues that pilfery funds
By way of hijacked tax revenues,
Of a people who no longer stammer
As endearingly as Jimmy Stewart,
You American in Pimlico,
You snubbed by Pimlicoans,
Superior to them who are
Part living dead, part Druid, and we,
        We haven't even got to the poets, yet.
Let Hawking the cosmologist hawk his wares,
His soup-tin tenor acquainting us
With tomorrow's tenure,—
The only event horizons that maintain your interest,
Speaking of singularities and waves and Euclid,
Are the promise of her thighs, the steady-state smile,
                the unfathomable eyes of a terrorist
                who could have sex on the brain
                        but more likely seeks
                a leg-up in the culture wars.
                        But where was I? Ah, yes.

Eric, put yourself back in your child's mind
        When you were not yet a man-child—
Do you not see how it was,
 How mother-love and father-love availed you little,
As, of a sudden, the universe gaped,—ravenous maw
Ate galaxies, ate lilies, gulped salamanders
And Studebakers, swallowed entire

West and east Beirut and all of Iowa
     In a waking dream?

There you were, a rubber-kneed miscreant.
(You will have had an accident in your shorts.)

There you were, expecting punishment.
Bewildering then—mom's tinkling laughter,
 Your distress her comic relief, so much so, that as you looked
Into the grim eyes of God, you didn't fade,
Just that the sky disappeared, even the idea of sky,
And the trees and flowers and grasses and the family pooch,
Some hulking, guardian mountain at the limits
     Of human dominion—poof, all gone.

And yet, in the way one played at cowboys and Indians
And put up with the incongruous laughter of a mother
And the larking of playmates,
One has spent the rest of one's life so far
Resurrecting presences, even their evils as when
Rebels are lynched in the shade of oaks
And Christ, like Shakespeare, is subject
     To seminars, the hunt on
     For the meaning of our mystery smiles.

For yes, new breeds of barfly will swill new concoctions
And assuage fresh rounds of prejudice.
And then, that elderly Roman there
On the via Giacinto Carini, he'll have occasion to stoop,
To inspect pavement, and how grand
The immensity of that dog loaf, one worthy
     Of a triumphal arch.

We'll have ourselves new rights and wrongs
Such as draw missiles, shells and bullets,
Just as weddings bring flowers,
Just as funerals attract bouquets.
And yet another horror passes
    And the dead move on.

Doom Past Cure

Lunar, what with the heat and the girls in dresses,
What with the beer and the salted nuts,
The terrasse biblical and pagan in the dark of the evening,
As some ancient towns had been—like Antioch,
My friend Labrosse was bewildered,—he was glassy-eyed
Who figured he knew it all and knew his limits,
   And how it's gone and where it's headed, he in his 67th year.

But if a mature body had heart for mam'selles
And would frolic with them and fool around
And drink in a somewhat pedantic manner,
A mature mind couldn't overlook
Panic in the eyes of happy women:
    So many good works in the heart-sack of a man.

For Labrosse the unbeliever was bending back in his mind
To the old religion he never really relinquished:
The necking, the petting, the kisses galore,
René Lévesque and Pierre Trudeau, Firebirds with shiny wheels,
Camus and lakeside cabins, his deepest thoughts on these subjects
    Charmingly slurred.

Well, the girls who attended to Labrosse last night
And suffered their favourite man-child without complaint,
Might save us, yet, their worlds, in any case, offering them
Pleasant viewing, their worlds wide picture windows
Through which they have only to step and shiver
To the thrill of touches exotic and familiar:
Infatuation, heartbreak and the cold realities of the cold hand
      Of the marketplace.

Their eyes spoke yes to the give and take
  Of boy-girl affections, bare shoulders sumptuous
And inviolate, bare toes innocent of killing fields
      And slush funds and who knows what.
      A pretty picture, one almost true.

But enough. You, Lunar, you continue listless.
I, without hope, read Greek tragedies.
And bad goes to worse and love's a word
  One oughtn't discount or lavishly praise
While the atoms dance, while we strap on
Each our harness of necessity as those atoms lark,
      And doom arrives as deliverance.

Yankee Boy in Baseball Gear

Can you stand to hear it, Eric, how
                              the yankee boy in baseball gear,
His mitt dangling from the handlebar,
Pedalled the bike through the potato field
    Under the migratory thunder cloud? How he was on the way to the army base
From Wallstadt where he lived, ancient hamlet that curdled the nose
                              with coal and sour milk and beer,

with pigshit, with sweet confections,
and the nitrous odour of
war bride bitterness
not far from Heidelberg, near Mannheim
that was terror-bombed in '41?

He was, just then, in unsupervised time,
An independent agent of the occupation, so much so
They were seeing a vision—those old women of loamy acreage,
beasts of burden, friendly hags
of toothless and cracked smiles.

It had rained, and the precocious boy,
knowing as he did
(even before he could hardly know)
That it was a lesson in Roman history, his being there,
That it was *Germania*, that it was he who could will that the sun should shine
As he loved the game of baseball, was aching to play, that evening,
Hoping against hope there'd be no rainout,
the parents quarrelling, father in his cups
who'd love one and all and everybody
and Mario Lanza, good-time tenor.

And the women, somewhat tickled
With the boy's presumption, for all that he was an American
who could boss the sun around,
Were amused, smiles all the more cracked and pungent.
(Simple agricultural spirits, hey, Eric, and this not so long
After the horrors of the war?)

In their voluminous skirts,
Scarfed and aproned, they were

hunkered to the sod,
       so many sunflowers there,
As if they themselves were the products of a seed,
Black earth tangy from rain, the light of the sun
Straining to gain purchase, the boy in league with the rainbow's
 Glimmer.
Some of the women raised their arms
     to this their hierophany of a lad,
And he, he may as well have been Adonis for
All those weathered faces, crones whose inner imps
   were Aphrodites of a river's plain.

Too much the narrative for you—the words above?
As if Tacitus and *The Katzenjammer Kids* were of the same
Mind, not to mention the hangover, the regrets
 In light of history's most destructive conflict—

Even so, the memory of it now and then
Rears up from where memories bide their time
Patiently, in anticipation of doing their worst,
And what *was* now simply *is*: a pastoral, a piece
Of bucolic legerdemain, as were you and your outback
 And the smell of ozone after a storm.

§

Renderings from Propertius

as Delivered to Gaston Côté

I

So long as my synapses fire, so long as you have an ear
And it's willing, receive then what tumbles by:
Cause and effect and their love-child farce.
Let it not pass unheralded, let it not be overlooked
How she hazed me there in the library,
Her walk a slow and meditative walk,
Thoughtful essay, time, space and motion explained.
She gave her all to this lecture, and there were going to be exams,
Her unconcern cruel, her sweet and gentle eyes
Made sweeter and gentler in their myopic sweep
By the lenses through which they took in
                    her world. She meant no harm.
And yet, no chin was more imperious, her flashing nails sirens
Calling out to lovesick sailors in the stacks, Propertius just a name on a shelf,
                              Nixon not yet gone to China.
The ring on her finger said weddedness
And for all I ever knew it was fine by her
Who suffered no complications of guilt or remorse, 9 to 5 a necessity
                              punctuated by caresses.
Can't say who she most liked to read, if she read at all.
Why discuss Proust when her kisses took
        their prisoners, her clinch absolute
There against some wall by the fire alarm?
But all that was then, is perhaps overblown
In my memory-bank, small balance that has since
                    bulged with interest, ballooned
Into a fair-sized chunk of change, so much so I hear now

Eve Tremblay: "Monsieur, you were a pleasant way
To solve my boredom." I was, in any case, too poor for love
And she too much of something else to honour
            an impecunious condition with amour.
Yes, Gaston, it's pathetic, as the cars of an evening slick
Over the rain-slicked street, as the leaves fall and life's a tease,—
As passersby, bending to the wind and rain, are the stuff
Of routine, desire cold and large out there,—
As we sit in a café that would be Greek
And lets the sorry likes of us hang about,—
To know that what were shadows then
Are shadows now. And she was a loon,
And I a clown, still.

II

Club your opponents senseless with gist.
Rattle position papers.
No matter. Oceans rise and other menace
Occurs. Libraries go bust, and one suspects
Public intelligence is a ghost of itself.
Nothing to be done about what follows, to wit
We are each of us so many clown spots hanging out
On a clown's body. We twist in the wind
At the behest of a ringmaster's whip hand.
What's more, bliss was always a mad hound, but we knew it was madness,
Just that, bliss is all curled lip, too, Gaston.
And it's snarl and it's bark, and it stalls for time.
And, here in the café, winter on tap, light at premium,
You drink now so as to drown
The shrill tenor of my voice.

III

You've been out on a toot, Gaston, a company do.
You've come home. Your darling's asleep.
She's beautiful there in her dreamland, all cares
          disappeared from her angelic face.
And yet, though you would like to take license,
Would steal a heartfelt smooch, you can't—
She outclasses you, and five will get you ten she'd only get
Umbrageous, as she wakes and would smell on your person
Some other person, all the while you sniff her dreams
          for your replacements or her hissy fits.
          Ring any bells? Is this what you miss,
As you sit here at table now, years after the fact,
Monastic, chary of love, restless,
You a number that some demographic specialist
               crunches
So as to get a handle on the libido of the aging male?
Gaston, drinking buddy, worldly-wise,
You let me believe one thing while the truth is else,
Or that you never philandered, and you were unprepared
For your honeymoon night. Go on, tell me another.
But were you drunk or were you sober,
Were you as free of sin as any newborn mark
Come into the world to be someone's supper,
When, no virgin now, you let yourself in the house, the door familiar,
She was indifferent to this miracle of a faithful husband,
And she simply rolled over, showing you her
Skeptical nature.

IV

Odds are, Gaston, they'll say
We died for nothing and lived for less.

59

We might as well have pinched her suburban arse,—
We might as well have run for mayor or else.
So, what with that black cloud roiling above,
What with those sidewalk leaves whipped about,
The passing sky of crows and our ephemeral clout,
Our little accomplishments so many vanities
That, deep down, we hope no one really notices, we're sunk
In time's passage, that troubled promenade
            on the deck of a wave-tossed ship.
Such specialists we were meant to be, what *wunderkind*,
And how we were going to change the world, and we did,
And did we ever, and now it's damn near hopeless,
Too much body at the expense of spirit.
Then again, a look in her eye, a smile within her, and
It was always love: she a flower clinging to her stone desert,
Commonplace of metro, bus or elevator.
And when philosophy is put to pleasure, religion is next,
                and how you hate all that plumage—
So then pour, just pour, and I'll overlook for now
That, though you'll try, though you'll make a manly effort,
      you're the prose that can't keep at bay
      a world that wants poetry to fade away.

V

Effect, Gaston, follows cause
In almost every transaction nature permits.
Or else we must assign to pixie sand,
To angel dust or subprime mortgages
The power, the incapacitating capacity
To upset precedent, and fantasias cavort
Without penalty, the galactic ballroom a pleasure dome now
                        to a fresh round of realists.

60

In any case, Gaston, bemuse your demons, ask yourself
Why the rules of the house dishearten us.
You might hear it's life itself, not parliament
That validates blowhards and zealots, all of whom ride
The slipstreams of vested interests. (Now note that the wine we drink
                    leads to crushing certainties, the café a kind
                              of technical institute—)
Then ask the man who would know another man's wife,
Who would covet a garden and get a desert
Of satin sheets: "Sir, when, at the wire, comedy and tragedy are neck and neck,
Can melodrama triumph at dark horse odds?"
I suppose that, in your books, if there be a God,
He's Pure Logic, has no truck with what's absurd,
And if there is no god then nature is sense, the how and why
Of all that transpires—our no-nonsense dominion then,
With or without influence-peddling, pure serendipity
              the integrity of our orbit around the sun,
              and from desire spring the besetting difficulties.
                              Sound about right?
Gaston, I've loved and hated for two thousand years,
So I know there's no point in begrudging you
What excites you most. Your cherished priority?
To seal a porous pot through which reason drips,
You sweet on the sweetest of temptations—
                    an iron-clad case.

VI

Otherwise, Gaston, yes, if you say so:
You love verse, love it to bits. You love it as much as you love
Steak and wine, as you love women beyond your reach.
Well, as they say, I smell a rat. Not even poets
Cherish the thing so ardently, and twice

On the day of rest. No, not as much as you do,
　　　　you humanist with business credentials—
You secured, a bachelor now, Gaston Côté is sitting pretty,
Quebec's little revolution an outgoing tide.
I suspect a liberal's sense of guilty guile
In your zeal for art, panic, too.
What if this crazed poet with whom you drink
　　　　　　　and mark most evenings
With your objections to his pessimism, what if he knows a thing or two,
　　　　　　　　　is right about what he says comes for us,
　　　　　　　　　　new world orders easy come easy go?
　　　　　Then let me speak on Tremblay, please,
　　　　　　　before this order unravels.
　　　　　　　—And here she is, silver Christmas bells affixed
　　　　　　　　　to her form-flattering sweater—
She signals me to meet her in the poetry stacks,
　　　　safe from busybodies and our bosses.
She would pick my brain for ruses, she at wit's end
As husband wishes to whisk her to some vile place
For the holidays. "Lie," I say. "Plead allergies. Or else, suffer him."
Yes, not to be borne—winter golfing in Florida.
Right then and there we get down to cases
There in the broom closet, and it's as if she and I, in our kisses,
Each leave our mark on the body of love, the one hallooing to the other
Throughout the course of time. Epic silliness.
But then, Gaston, isn't this what you wish to hear,
　　　　that love-body with its insoluable dramas
　　　　　　ineffably more to the point
　　　　than any science, religion, voting bloc
and other tweedledumdee? Well, you're not sure—
　　　　　Winter golfing? It wasn't so bad.

VII

I said, "Look, Gaston, about Eve, why, you don't think we actually did it,
Rutting in the poetry stacks—there with Propertius and Wallace Stevens,
Bringing blushes to the cheeks of beatnik scribes? Can't believe you believed me—"
You answered: "Not so fast. I always allow, as business taught me to allow,
For certain dissimulations, bendings, if you will, of fact,
Hidden agendas, unsavoury purposes, and in your case, well,
Poets lie, if only because who takes them seriously?
But I respect endeavour: even you rate a hearing.
And as you're in the business of immortalizing me, I pay the tab—
The least I can do: maintain a steady flow of wine.
And if, in your ears, you seek out the echoes
Of the kisses of all the Eves, so much the better for my cause:
                                        it keeps you interested.
But if you think that the hatreds and the circuses,
The greed and stupidity that are doing in America
Will grab more than their fair share of my attentions, think again.
What did you expect? Nothing's forever. Everything changes.
Chances are, things will change back
To the old talking points of your grade school books.
And just to show you I'm a sport, don't need to carry
                every argument, it's yours, the last word."
"Hell's bells, Gaston, how nice you are to me. The wine's mellowed you,
                or else you've had your fibrillator tuned."

VIII

Yes but, we kissed and they paraded—shameless Propertian concoctions,
                barely remembered deities
Of summer sun and winter hearth-fire,
Of unappeasable wants, so much so,
                they vouchsafed
                continual research.

Or say it was autumn, the trees red, the pavements plastered
With leaves, the air almost tangy on account
Of the sweet-rot smell of fallen foliage,
And we, returned to ourselves, would go out,
Grappa and ice cream on the horizon,—
And Gibbon kicked in, or I.F. Stone
And what was playing at the odeon.
And it's only now, and I can't say why,
That I look to carve a valentine
On what time had been.

IX

Those who came back and then fell away
And so, they may as well have been body-bagged,
Were what gave me pause. Sure, they could tell you straight to your face—
Young-old boys not liking manhood—what they'd seen and what
They'd done, and speak of the enemy as a force of nature.
And yet, sometimes, a shift in tone said more
About what'd been service and what was reward,
And a terrible rage reduced to whispers was witness
To a kind of whipped dog bewilderment in the eye,
    and you heard: *it wasn't supposed to be this way.*
As for me, you'd think that forty some years is long enough,
Should suffice for making of lines of verse
That, as they stand, are far from adequate treatment
Of a debacle. Truth to tell, I often dismissed
    the *"Pssst, hey pal, I've got a story for you,*
        but damn it all if I know what it is."
And so, the Billys and Whitakers and other wretches
Who stared into space, who scowled, who barely stomached
A know-nothing like myself, may have, at last, in old age got
Their home-field advantage, their civilian death and burial.

X

Why so curious? You ask me now in what I believe.
I answer: "Not in God, not in humankind.
In love, perhaps, which some will argue
Is part God's and part humankind's.
(As to the rest of the animals I can't say,
Nest-love something else again.)
And I endeavour, as should you,
To keep this and other questions open:
So much out there would draw the curtains
And make of every question a *been there, done that* trifle.
And now, to clear up another matter:
Was she so very gorgeous, a time-stopper?
Of course. Would a poet lie about such a thing?
But all that, to be sure, was years ago—
Memory is such a vagabond teller of tales.
The absolute is staring us in the face.
What's stopping you, man?
Why don't you pour?"

XI

"From where does the poetry come?" you ask.
"Is there in your mind a machine that churns
Out creation?"And I put it to you, "No, but listen,
                    if she laughs, laughter's my muse.
She wears blue jeans, then verse is denim.
Say she shows up in a dress and heels,
And now she'll gladhand a tone-y crowd,
Well then, a poem that's known too much dog and pony
And pretends it hails from the provinces,
          agog with the turn of her ankle,
          she rating ardor on a sliding scale,

Just might honour how she's nature's jewel.
How else would it be, my brain—nature's jest—
No mind of Zeus spewing forth perfections?
The genius is not me—it's there, out there,
  in the colour of the trees, be it fall.
Autumnish, yes, and I know I'm mortal.
What's more, there are lovers who never learn.
What's more, there are souls who have to make do
With a single instance of an embrace,
Love made again and again, always."

XII

Gaston, just so you know, I was intimate with the jealousies.
     You needn't sit there smug.
Now you may understand that I, too,
Conspired against myself like this:
An hour with her and I knew that after
I'd burn in an arsonist's handiwork.
There'd follow days of agonies, and still more
Until she thought me prime for the next conflagration,
The next round of a groaning prick,
And if she got bored, well then, I'd renew her interest
Which wasn't so difficult—It was said that to look on a god
Invited a contract on one's existence.
Can't tell you how many times I beheld
Cupid's insipid, jeering mug
As I saw myself in her arms
And kissed a thousand hallucinations.
   All the more galling for his being a punk
Who'd gall you even more, pouring gas on the fire, blowing his ta-ta's
At your wretched state.
     Worse than dashed hopes as when

New blood fails in office, the country in vertigo
          from the spiralling down to ruin,
     and barring the ache for the loss of one dear,
Is to watch what was yours now claimed by another
In the fires of love. And then, and here one smacks one's head
As sentience creeps up one's neck, one inquires,
"What did one have that was only a mirage
Of craven bliss, and we've yet to speak of love?"
There it is then. Clink my glass. Gloat, if you must.
But the longer you will continue to insist
All's well, and if not, it'll turn around,
Why then, I'll just have to genuflect
At your MBA, won't I, Gaston,
That *ne plus ultra* of the mind.

XIII

I put one foot ahead of the other,
And in love with life, ambulated, the autumn air delicious
On my old face. Leaves fell to the street.
If a moral nature derives conscience
From indifferent nature, squirrels plumed
All over the place, were cheeky buggers
On the young bark of the young maples
Shedding their red-gold attitudes.
Then pigeon-birds, filthy, obsessed, but friendly-like,
Like so many dolphins on the pavement, escorted my progress
Past the little park, that one shaped like an arrowhead,
          and I looked and saw no slackers
     tethered to young boughs by their own intestines,
               and it seemed good news.
And a woman with high cheekbones made
Bawdy eyes my way, and in love with life, I was tempted.

No doubt, she thought me mature, broken-in,
This Phaedra intolerant of moody, if prettier youth.
Let me say it again: either pitch your verse at the highest
Pitch, or, chaste as a child playing at jacks,
    get down and dirty, all else the burbs.
                In any case, I breezed along.
To keep it brief, Gaston, and though Zeus philandered
                 and Apollo chased
Daphne to the ends of the earth, and Hippomenes outsmarted Atalanta
And got this athlete of a girl, and all these were tales with versions,
               poetry in its infancy,
      the Romans who salinized Carthiginian earth
          were as modern as Agent Orange.
Now have you heard the latest, how it is the generals
    have put their heads together, and would catapult
        one of their own in the White House
        and there could be Julius Caesar to pay?
No? Well, the wind blew. The leaves tumbled down.
       My eyes clouded with slate-black cloud.
There are other worries besides politics in life:
      A dog whined, deeply worried that
      darling master might fail to emerge
from happy hour in the Four Aces Bar.

XIV

I hear you: Gaston wants that his wine be drink,
Not swill watered down with social commentary.
My muse is addled, he says: war, love, lust, Caesar,
      the shenanigans of the financial sector.
    Why, they're all over the place—these verses,
As if I were some shorebird, long-legged bundle of nerves
                and aversions

Who finds the shore unstable, the tide treacherous, too many
                              gawking tourists about
              looking for spirituality in the flaming sunset
              and I can't settle anywhere on the beach.
                              Gaston has a point.
So why don't I snap my fingers and dancing girls appear,
              and failing that, Sinatra, Gaston happy
                      in his rotarian appetites?
But credit me this: at least I don't game the system
With the obscenities of special appeals. I say a thing and it's said,
                      Seven Types of Ambiguity be damned.
              No net made of language ever captured much,
                      or else poets would be Stalins.
My love affairs? Disasters, mostly. And for this, I blame
Myself, and though the ladies soldier on with perfect egos,
              it does seem in accordance with nature's design.
My pessimism?
              Now here's a product of experience.
My faith?
              It's Homer the bard. Enough said, just that
If we assume, on account of our greater knowledge, we've given
              the old tragedies the slip, then what fools we are.
Yes, Gaston, pour, yes, if only for comedy's sake,
      that divorcée three tables over making eyes
          with you in mind—shall I make inquiries?

XV
So what is it, Gaston, you come in out of sorts
On a Sunday afternoon? Too much football? Too much golf?
Too many silver-tongued sportscasters, their throats sounding brass?
Yes, what spectacle most maintains the illusion
              that all is ordered, peaceful, prosperous,

and justice, for the most part, carries the day
Than the perfect addressing of a dimpled white sphere,
No matter that, as it soars, it hooks wildly right
      and then burrows into some hazard,
      and dignity requires that a contender
          grin and bear it?
I was sitting here minding my own business,
And you enter the café in a bearish temper,
And you plunk down the wine as if this action
      were a call to battle. You say,
     "Maybe, just maybe, you're right", and then
      your voice tails off. Unusual, seeing as
         you always win your point.
Damn it all, what's got you by the short hairs?
Ah, you've read the latest poll. Now Gaston knows
Americans have no great regard for their government.
Well, knock me over with a feather: there's revolution
      just around the corner.
Ah, it's women. So then, time for first things first—to cut a rug
      with a grey-haired lovely or two,
     all limbs creaky and arthritic. Seems ghastly.
Even so, what's stopping you? It's not for me to come between
      a man and bliss,—
Not for me to tut-tut ladies when in their eyes
     they get those imps.
Or that the voice of wisdom says, as it should:
"What wisdom? The well-ordered mind, in dubious times,
      wearing poncy clothes, striding manfully
from green to green with a bag of lightning-conductors,
     sizes up his lie and selects his weapon.
      If the cities must burn, they'll burn.
     But I, for one, lack this harmonious blend

Of thought, purpose, execution, which is why I sit here
               and imbibe and review the histories
       And hear out a professional like yourself.
                For when you blink I figure
                     it's significant."

XVI

Incoming—silks and spices. Outgoing—torrents of silver.
And that's how it was for cottagers
Whose villas were so many altars to Aphrodite
       in the sun-splashed years of the empire.
But, Gaston, as you might wish to know,
What has the trade imbalance of Rome
         to do with Robert Zimmerman's
            It's All Over Now, Baby Blue?
            The cost ratios of desire?
               Mazel tov?
            The death of sentience in
       those who might've valued it most?
Two months shy of the winter solstice and the shortest day,
One's serotonin reserves at peril (if one is conscientiously
               upwardly mobile, not a working stiff),
It may be observed, nonetheless, that winter's struck
And this or that darling shall be drifting south
To splay toes in the tide-darkening sand,—
To count the suns and count one,—
To count the moons and count dream-love
Though one will have understood
That where there's love there's cost,—
To count the stars and endearingly assume
They are numberless, so many alternate scenarios up there
        to the drama-queen mind of humankind.

Naked and silhouetted by light,
Stepped out of the shower, her towel a headdress,
She did not stop my heart—she rendered it superfluous,
      and I was spirit in the presence of a goddess,
           unaccountably inarticulate,
     love of man for woman and woman for man—
       love in general pegged to wherewithal.
        I trust, Gaston, that you are acquainted—
surely, you are acquainted with love's mysteries—
       as are pegged to ways and means,
      you no stranger to boardrooms
     though you've been otherwise chaste.
     That I amuse you tells me you are amused,
Even if, in the sounder regions of your mind, you sound off:
     "These poets—they will fly in the face of the evidence,
        but then I guess that's why they're poets.
          There's no other explanation."

XVII

That nipping wind from northern parts,
That pack of girls on the run in darkness,
Fleeing classes, fleeing the job, home and its horrors,
      announce the end of summer light.
          Pour, Gaston, just pour.
I must say it fascinates—how you, schooled
In the fray that was business, politics, marriage, divorce,
Deal with the fact you no longer rate,
The world more corrupt than when you set out
To achieve, tomorrow's thin winter sun
Your pencilled-in applause.

XVIII

The male of our species is the problem, Gaston,
And the least savoury among us were handed a gift
        when women declared trust annulled.
            Why should a jerk learn to care?
Otherwise, as an ancient poet had it, Caesar bringing the empire glory,
There's only hanging out on the boulevard, fresh from the exertions
                                of the bed,
While wheeler-dealers, while soldiers are catching
            honour for their efforts
To render the world safe for yet more bonanzas.
In this way is lust the ironist, and in the sport
Men and women are one another's equals, and equally cynics.
Yes, here's a conundrum no one seems able to solve:
What makes for free spirits, one day, enslaves the next.
I've stood on the Sacred Way, tipping my flat cap
At the ghosts of men, women and exotic animals,
Listening to touts carving business from business,
Hearing out the senators, their glory second-hand,
This or that sun at its zenith,
This or that moon a caution,
Ruin in the corner of my eye,
And then it's in your face.

XIX

American rustic leaves me indifferent.
What simpler, nobler, more virtuous life?
What use have I for prairie sod? They are pretty pictures in my schoolboy's
Mind—New England groves splendid and haunted
        with Puritan sex and dead Indians.
For every good cowboy were there not
        ten pistol-packing psychopaths?

No, city slicker, alleged poet to boot,
I'm chary of nature and human nature. The sacramental drink,
The harvest toast, the self-congratulatory nod
Was spilled blood. So then, Gaston, pour the wine. Don't stint
                       as I'm only just getting started.
For who knows who squeezed the last Etruscan tear,
           Rome making good on her takeover bid?
     They are still crying in the Seven Cities of Gold.
              Humankind will wander and trespass,
               and in this way generate conflict,
         and each beseiged tribe will have its prophet,
            and among prophets contention,
        arguments as to the best course of action
                  in a slew of troubles:
        a return to the old ways? Making it new?
In these parts, decimation is still an answer of sorts,
          Fortress America an open-air crypt
             of crumbling infrastructure
          and advanced weapons systems.
        "No comment," you say. I don't see why,
      the relations of your forebears to the Iroquois
        complicated, begging for commentary,
              all that raid and counter-raid,—
      and then the beaver almost disappeared.
           Still, who needs obligatory outrage?
    Who wants to be reminded of ancient history?
          Just that I have superstitious respect
            for ghosts and cycles of retribution.

XX

They were smug and corrupt, he said
And so, he tossed his hat in the ring,
And he'd boot the bums from their cosy offices,

And if I meant him no ill will, truth to tell, I was skeptical.
                              He answered:
            "Yes, and that's what they figure you for,
        That you've had your brush with experience.
                    You'll stay at home on voting day
                And they'll live to dance the beguine."
                              Gaston, he shamed me.
And his sombre sidekick (her eyes sweet and alive, what with the way
She held her clipboard and seemed attentive)
Had the look of a woman for whom
Civilization had reached its eleventh hour,
And I was proof, if nothing else,
Of how bankrupt it had all become,—
And either she'd buzz a thousand more doors
Before the night was done, or she'd let down her hair
                    and cave to long-denied indulgences.
I'd never know, the man with conviction in his jaw,
Sensing perhaps that her unspoken questions
Spoke more to me than his reforms,
Broke off relations, and they moved on.
I returned to the ballgame on TV, old rite of passage,
To the pretense of America at its best, everything in a nutshell—
                              truth, honour, justice—
Swings and misses, absolutely smoked, the intricate physics
                    of what was a boy's paradise,
                    big money boondoggle now.
Gaston, I shrugged as I lay on the couch, observed athletes, heard out shills,
And I was a body within a body that, with aplomb,
Could still throw and catch and keep at bay
Lies, collusion, loveless nights,
Collective madness,
Marauding death.

XXI

Stick me on some flood plain of the world
And set loose the waters of the record,—
And then, to further addle a metaphor,
Grant me the expertise of a connoisseur
Who, by taste alone, can trace a grape
To its locale,—and I might observe as I sample
          this wave or that inundation:
            'Clovis' or 'pre-Clovis' people,
     this or that variation on a genetic theme,
   but don't expect a grand summation of what
   it all means. Shall we, Gaston, drink to that?
The thing is, I'm at an impasse—I just can't see a way
To end this writing on a decent note
Save for squawk, bleat or howl of protest
       deliverable, as ever, to the geist,
          that one whose holistic spas
Sanction torture, excuse mediocrity, and in everything—
       from making a buck to making art and love—
          reduce endeavour to paint-by-numbers,
     and what happened to those Mayans, anyway?
So I'll step outside, if you don't mind—I'll light a cigarette
And sniff the wind for an ill wind,—I'll contemplate
         your suspect career and mine,
   as well as those of the duped darlings of the day.
The clouds above—there's snow in them, and this time around I resent
That skinflint sky stingy with light, and yet,
Were I to hop a southbound plane and find myself
          in Quintana Roo,
     clambering over vine-clad temples,
   I'd feel a fraud, one too clever by half,

looking to apply the old mismanagements
to the narcissisms of shopping malls.
Besides, there's more honour getting drunk with you here
yes, in this faux-Greek café
than there is in flashing a credit card
in a real Cozumel.
But enough of the interlude, my self-involved spell.
Gaston, I'm back at you, and I see you've poured,
you cupbearing straight man,
you tutoring Silenus.
You see, something like inspiration hit me out there,
And I have it now: how a wanton muse to an ancient poet
Shall get the last word and get me the note
I've been looking to strike, and she'll fly
On dream-feet, she'll fly from her grave to the poet's couch.
And in no uncertain terms, she'll let him know what a bastard he is.
Even so, she'll say she likes the verses he writes her.
But will he see to it that her slaves, beloved companions
To her love-crimes, about to retire from a career of intrigue,
Are well-cared for? And then, and it's either a touching
Or a grisly coda, she'll remind her old adversary in the love-wars
That when he joins her in death, bone against bone,
They'll embrace, once again, and forever.

§

Tirade and Fluff, for Foulard

I

Foulard, you're next on my list
Of interlocutors who want their sense,
What with these windy metres of mine, the world
All bomb and blast and bombast, philosophical mewings and worse.

Yet, what have we to talk about? An ocean parts us.
Your down-at-heels nation-state tries not to gloat
Over my alma mater down in the mouth,
Snake-bit, war-maddened, its parts
But jailbait for the banks, morally, spiritually, intellectually spent,
Not to put too fine a point on it. Need I go on?

Then again, are we not poets, knights to the good,
Chivalrous in armour of linen and straw,
Aging rhymesters whose reward
For passions, street creds, amorous wooing of love,
Is to rate hothouses of the Absurd,
Drunkeness, spite, herniated souls?

Shall we talk it up, in any case, how we're isolate
In our skins, like all hosers of middling realms, we perhaps
Not uncomfortably adrift in our Babylonian phase of unease,
Harps strung for satire and plunging tears?

Rightly, we viewed with suspicion the Big Idea,
The Big Vision, the Siren's sweet panacea,
Some Mao pitching dark shadows against
The dark shadows of a cave, mayhem at hand
To make of every flower a weed without face—

Such old news, just that the capitalist ethos,
Once a way of life, has supplanted life itself.
(The pay-off? Gadgetry. Fetishes. Stars on ice.)

Now I hear Clytemnestra in stealth-prayer,
The branch of a blossom-tree scraping her bedchamber,
Madness steeling itself to take on madness, business as usual:
Sacking Troy, tripping home to brag and liaise with the wife.

You working-class hero, you trollop with laptop,
What with your lush art critique, your astringent verse,
If you can't hear what I hear, can you see what blinds me—
That so much of life is written in stone?
That in the Sweepstakes of Ruin Bush wins hands down
Over Caligula and his designs on Rome?

In any case, receive these lines, pitiful stuff,
With your usual good manners. Be kind.
And Bob's your uncle. And something's gaining,
The world all laughing rapine.

II

Demagogues blove and punch-drunk moms
Slip on the silky stuff of truth in politics
As they might slip on sex out in the sticks
And acquaint the locals with gravitas.

And then, calamity, and one can't figure
How the disasters come, nature mum in these matters
As when the good Germans began to sing
Those sickening-sweet songs of their self-love—

I biked often to the old student town,
Stopping this side of the Roman bridge
That, like some dull-witted monster on a toot,
Would wade the river. The boy I was
Looked for God in the clouds above Heidelberg.

And amidst the glittering dragonflies that stitched
Together a tapestry of time and its parts,
Something registered, something frightened, how it is
Each day reaches for the one that's next.

Two bits to see *Lolita* back at the base.
It was free, the whores and the GIs just over the highway—
In another sovereignty—haggling amiably enough
At the gas station by the beer-stocked cooler—

—*As if any of it can be solved*—
—*I was imperial at the age of twelve*—

III
If love can't unseat the facts of life,
Facts can't undo love's little triumphs,
That Chrome Edition with nickel-plated reeds
Tucked in his hand, his beery breath sucked in.
To my delight, he conjured for me
The long, long freight trains whistling by
The Virgilian arbors of hot afternoons,—
Engineered the Apollonian gloom of storm skies,
The yellow lightnings of a state of mind,—
All the Golgothas, all the hot potato baseballs
In the deep shade realms of Missouri oaks,—

Sour green apples, glassy arachnids,
Black walnuts, twig-like insects,
Skittering locusts, the grass knee-high—

§

That Little Matter of the Cherub Addressed

I

There being no end to the illusions,
There being the immeasurable persuasions
Such as dictate to the universe its laws
And its mirages, even her smile,—

There being one's secret wants
That are as everyday as pepper and salt
(And has she not pepper and has she not salt
And her oracles of desire beyond counting
That go pop morning, noon and night?),

All that then remains to love
For the making right of things, and she has right to make
From all the wrong that's been vouchsafed,
Is empty ceremony, the pieties of
Idol and smoke, reason a bust, the intellect failed,
She still in it for the soul.

II

And she imagines she honours the soul
When she accords the world a pass and takes
Vacations from it, war and profit and right behaviour
Forgotten a while, and she reads
How the ancient harp was once
Our sweet childhood,
If not our innocence.

Would she accept a song from me
Were I to strike a happy resonance
With something made of tortoise shell
On the periphery of extinction?

III

And she imagines she enables love
When she schemes a conquering love, when she'd have
Witches and magi and tricksters,
Princesses and princes of truth,
And stammering kids afraid of the dark,
Queue up to dance to her heartache tune
That is justice in her own image.

IV

Oh, she has an healthy appetite, she who eats like a modest psyche
In a panic. And by now she will have eaten,
As she is a far-ranging forager in the world,

Her truffles in Verona, Italy, her vichyssoise in New Orleans,
Her baked Alaska in Seattle. And the bill of fare in Kuala Lumpur?
Dog or goat? Strange artichoke? Ah, tandoori, then ritalin,
And quite apart from our cuisine, tons of margarine,
New grotesqueries being Syrian
Of the regime of Assad,
Whereas, with Americans, what's grotesque is nothing new,
Of the regime of 'my bad'—

Moreover, she will say her parents love her,
The saying so so much braggadocio.
Will have had her legs spread on the settee,

And the parakeet cackle in its cage
That here's a darling girl,

And she will have dreamed at dawn,
No, she will have argued at the fatal hour of dawn
With God, or with no entity in particular,
That love can be better, can get no worse,—
That life is life everlasting,
But that it isn't the stuff
Of which the Christ spoke.

V

Yet, isn't the soul a beautiful thing, the way it swears out
Its warrants for its own arrest, as when it flees
Hot, airless rooms of nattering artists
Rigged with culture and charm, and lovable
Up to a point, as were one's liberal parents of old?

VI

The poets say, or they used to say—
When the air was pure, that old-time mountain tubercular air—
That passion completes the rose,
Gold the colour of the summum bonum,
Smoky-blue the sensualist's eyes,
And those are her sardonic eyes,
As there is so much in the dark
That truly frightens her.

VII

Look, she is the reason, the intellect, the hope
Made to order for suburban hellholes.

She is the empty ceremony, the pieties of idol and smoke
By which the bottom will reach for us   ·
With so much more alacrity than would've been the case
Had we sworn off the making of hope,
The making of love, the making of children—

VIII

So she has recourse to sex-crazed boys,
And none last beyond the sunrise hour,
And while she's kissed and fondled and treated
She contemplates pecans and creams

And how it is that dates in their palmfuls
Take the edge off the hole in her gut,—
How it is that lemon meringue
Pushes back every harangue,

The pumping of fists
At each and every celebratory hour
Saying, "Me, too, look, I triumph."
Well, who's going to be the first idiot to say,
"We're losing ground, and fast"?

IX

But then she, sleepy, even so, sees it:
Slow-motion dream of life unfolding,
And she unloved and not loving much
Because no one recalls the how and why of it.
Or that they say, or used to say,
When philosophy once honoured the poet, no less,
How it is passion completes the rose

Or else the rose makes good the urge,
Smoky blue eyes the colour of whimsies and
The sensualist's eyes, bliss hard to contemplate and yet,
There it is: property still of the ancient gods.

Young Methuselah by the Pond

I

Look you through a sparrow's eye, look, and what's to see?
Paradise, to be sure, a sparrow's deities.
So I, human, wrote in a fit,
When I thought that writing met
A human need—

So long ago, wasn't it, we knocked about
From one end of the world to the next?
And it was ripe for pathos, of a piece, and proud,
Variously friendly to seers of its sights.
The Kabul that roughed us up nearly did you in:
Fever of the body gave rise to vistas
In the circus of the brain.
Then India, with all its elephants, snubbed your God, and yet
You found your health or it found you, and back in life,
You recrossed half the world,
I in your slipstream.

Spain, and we knew Segovia, Franco on the make.
The republic fated, yes, the young thing fell.
A fine-feathered friend could not abide
The lone guitar, he who swore by Plato's sad tale:
Our world, because material, is suspect.
—*Damn it all*, Carruthers would say—

And the next thing we knew, and science told us:
Here were neutrons whizzing
From Picadilly to the Argentine,

By way of Poughkeepsie, Perth or Anchorage,
Whizzing in all of space.
And who knows what else was in the works, financiers
Dropping like beanbags from the sky,
Without one thin dime to their detested lives.

You, my pretty, thought to wear, though you always did,
A silhouette. London, and Beecham conducted
A mellow Berlioz.
You glowed, you radiated.
Why, you premiered there,
Something lovely in the audience.
Did not the poet in me adore you to bits
Even if I in the poet, more practical, had more sense?

All the while the headlines were full of this, how it was
A corporal was on the loose. *He orated*
To a mass. He helped to make of it an abyss,
Twitchy jackanape that he was—
Now these beautiful monsters, dragonflies,
Are so many jewels above sparkling moss,
And wind that ripples the copper-green revery
Sails one more autumn
Across a dreamy surface.
Perhaps leaves on the water spell your name.
Perhaps so many telegrams call out to Celeste.
In any case, it starts up again:
A chasm widens with mounting lack.
It annunciates, what mischief,
The next wholesale abdication of the heart.

II

In a catch-as-catch-can fashion, with what remains
To me of my wits, I attempt to recall things.
Poetry is surely not what it used to be.
Oh, to be sure, poetry is more or less itself.
It rhymes, it motors on, just that
It's the stuff of hostage-taking, extortion and—
Well, have I loved a woman since I loved you?
Do you mind?

Carruthers? Poor boy would say we'll know tomorrow,
And if not then, then the next tomorrow, you wait and see,
Where it is Atlantis sits—off Cuba
Or in the Roman lake, and in our minds
And in our souls, and in our hearts.
Poor boy would say we'll know tomorrow,
And if not then, then the next tomorrow, you wait and see,
What stuff gravity is made of,
Whether it's what God inserts
In our minds, in our souls,
In our cold, cold hearts—
This pleasant wind that breathes on leaves light in the water
Bends the lawn in which your grave keeps
To a faith, to the blind faith that you abide
In the shadow of a god.
Yes, I can just make you out, you saying:
"Oh well, in such-and-such a year I took my leave.
It was the year when Ike left office
And told us, in the leaving, to beware.
We did talk politics, didn't we?
I recall piques, distempers, all my distress

That you bore up under, all my loves born of whims.
Boxers, cops. An economist?
Crime writer, crooner, shrimper—
Was it so awful for you, dearest?"

Yes, and I see you as ever with
Your sapphires and pearls, that gleam in your blue-gray eyes
Now keen on the Kennedys.
Down at the house all your people gather
To honour your enduring legacy.
Who'd get to the bottom of what ails the world,
Who can't fathom what ails the world,
Who say all the usual things,
Right in all the usual ways—
This showcase bit of water, antediluvian slough
Around which you skipped as a girl with your darling dolls,
Is the slitted eye of a god, maples flaming
In godly thought, the blue jays blue, the birches white.
You were always as pretty as any bloom.
From one day to the next, we were cheap
With one another.

But how it puts me in mind of you, this eye of God,
What with its russets and limes, its citron shades,
What with the autumn it would show the sky.
More than once, three times, perhaps, your theories had
A thought for how to bring about my happiness.
They only surrendered to the voice
That spoke of the expense.
For all that, Vienna, Berlin, Rome,
Geneva and Paris, yes, and New York, and there

It was, how we saw ourselves: our 'blue period',
Our fine but pessimistic lovemaking, and all
The fine drinks that we were knocking back, and the world
Would incur the next ready-to-hand
Collapse.

III

This yawn that consumes me from head to toe
Is longevity, I suppose. And it is the brief
Duration of our love,
Art short and marriage long.
Or that, if the world must burn, in any case, you,
You'd bring to the dance, however unwanted,
The imperatives of flesh, *your imperatives.*
You were gone from us before it struck,
And, his City on the Hill all ashine, grinning Reagan with cowlick,
Rocked the union man back on his heels.
You thought me unworthy of the great affair
Between the U.S.A. and some dark destiny—
Well then, here's what I am, if you've got a minute,
And, God knows, you've got an eternity, to wit:
When the early mornings are not yet light
And they still have night-skins to sluff off,
Here I'll sit, sleepless, Old King Cole of song
With a ceremonial cigarette, knowing you're there—
Here's my dry, old heart fluctuating, pitter patter—
Fiddle, fiddle, fiddle, and twice fiddle fiddle—
With its thoughts of you.
Here my lizard-like organs of sight
Take you in and Herr Hitler's cheap charm, you remarking:
"Why? He's only a man like any other—seducible."

And I? Now at a hundred and twelve? Still under a spell?
Too old to live, too young to bugger off?
The disgrace—
We're doomed to believe what presents us
In the best of lights—
Yes, yes, yes, ten thousand times, I whisper your name.
I see again the architecture of sex:
Your legs held high, those precious knees,
That cascade of hair down to your breasts.
Blue jays and bugs and clouds and flaming trees,
This pond, this God-eye of it all, in fact,
Answer the question you always put to me
When, yet again, you were fed up:
And what has the point of our lives been?
The answer? Such a bore it would make me were I to trot out
Modern rigmarole, ancient truth.

> *The easing down of the sun / mimics what light is left in my eyes.*
> *A lone crow. Wispy cloud / in a flame-red quadrant of the sky.*
> *Prosperous folk hereabouts, the hills jewel-like.*
> *Down at the house, your people / are debating,*
> *Well, what to do with me,*
> *The last person alive to have received your kisses,*
> *My poems of no account to them—*

IV

Is it not a mercy that it slips our minds:
Shabby instances of one's failure to grasp
One's insignificance and one's grotesque ego,
Though yours, my lovely, was monumental,
A sparkling business, consummate prowess,

And I mean your best and worst self,
As, unlike so many of us, you had no middling self.
And I mean your daunting eyes—
Carruthers? He hated the lone guitar
Though he swore by the showcase harp—Handel's
Offering—in B Flat Major—andante allegro
Oh-oh-oh
Pork pie and ice cream what Carruthers ate
While he kept the beat, you in his bed—

The thought of you all bone and absent flesh—

The 70s,
        And one read reportage like this:
        Aldrich gassed the house, the woman,
        the dog, the bird, himself, and struck the match.
        But is gravity, after all, God catching His breath?

And just the other day, this little gem:

We wait for Tripoli to go down,
You, me, the Masters of the Ball,
And then it's back to our middling lot,
The pursuit of its wherewithal.

And for all the horrors that came to be, you always said
The worst was still to come,
Man, woman and child however mad,
A still point in every blow.
Does the flower in its silence
Hear its soul?

It's the last of the light for this sacred day,
As all days are sacred, and they're mostly obscene.
Down at the house your descendants gather
To worship Celeste and laud her memory.
Perhaps they'll remember to feed an old man.

Near the Missisquoi

I

You'll think me gobsmacked if I declare
I was born in all innocence on a summer day.
Everything still June lush and green,
It was, so my mother said, auspicious.
But if she checked me close for weird cloven hoofs
And saw there was nothing strange to fear,
She missed the disguise I would come to endure—
To go with the knobs at the sides of my head—
Of leaf, of mud and stone and twig, of purling snow,
Gifts of a changeable sky, and all those bugs I had not meant to kill
With my heavy brogues.

II

Now who's euphoric? Who's idiot enough
For all that hoopla, that dog and pony
But a too-low order of self-styled artist
For whom art is a party favour?
Sex, misery, filthy lucre
Are at the bottom of all thinking
And the rest is scheming. And light
With its long-nailed fingers claws
Across a sky
Bringing day—

III

Well, I was up all night with my Craven A's.
I, Jim Light, was deep in the grog,
Hearing out Mister Herr Ludwig van Beethoven
(I'm quite done with Iron Maiden).

I was open-eyed with those 'last quartets'
In which love is a most terrible grace.
It's love ripped from the gaze of a god
And turned every which way
Like a prism: cool godly bands of light that lit
All that's in me, be it there or not.
And life, give you joy of it, is all you've got
Even when it's wrong and hopeless.

IV

And you never want to let slip away
How a smile was the worth of deity
For all that she had her doubts about deity,
About love, about passion's products—

The nasty surprises of which spite is one.
You see, I knew, even if you could not know,
That I'd get around to her soon enough, how she, a love of mine,
Took a knife to him, the one for whom she wore a ring.

—*That cool dry hand I knew so well*
That put me to a stammering heat—

—*Those pink thunderclouds blooming over the hills*
Near the Missisquoi—that's how it was
When she reneged on our congress—

V

Sleepless mostly, whores brought me sleep
When I could tear my eyes from the look of things.
Otherwise there was only her, and she was Ida Blue
Who, out of boredom, laid with me

In a hay barn on a Woolworth's blanket,
In the back of my truck on her lunch break—
She working at the bank, she driving me wild
Because, of a sudden abruptly, new.
What if it had been me, her Grade A fella
That she got it in mind to flense? No, *his* wounds weren't deep,
But she cut him some, though,
Then drove him to Cowansville, he in shock,
Submitted herself to the cops, to the court and prison
As if she were submitting herself to reason,
And I left the area, went to study art.

VI

I had it in mind to paint, to document, create
Cows and horses and deer and birds
And piles of stones and knobby hills,
The plush clouds, the maple groves,
The unsuspected gods in them,—
And barns and tractors and decaying cars,
And Ida Blue, Ida in the nude out of some regard,
And paint not according to Ingres or Degas,
And yet from loving recollection—*good God,
I'm raving*—You know, dreams die. Dreams of doing go inert,
And memory is another fallen temple
And life is littered with fallen temples.
And I'd paint some woman, sure, in the end,
And I surely have done that, often,
And with some credit, so say a few.
But paint that one? Love fails. Hate dissolves in hate,
And there's all that can never be fulfilled.

VII

Toronto of a time—ah, art student days,
And we'd sit around the pubs, identify the wrong,
Talk up the right. Rebel times. We'd infuse in ourselves
Pan love of a pan-world. Oh, it was as bad as that,
How we flattered ourselves, paired off, convinced ourselves
Now we were tested in our values. I think not.
Ida, you see, didn't make-believe: it was real skin at which she hacked
In her philosophic rage: her husband's virtue drove her around the bend.
I wrote her letters that she, past caring, never read.
I was only a minor scene
In a play chock full of scenes—

VIII

If I used to paint the old ones dying,
It was because I was obsessed with pain,
The panic in a countenance
To which only oblivion answers.
You don't see clever people hurting, do you?
I'm not so clever, I suppose, though I'm a walking costume ball,
Ghostly night at the ghostly vaudeville hall,
Leaf, twig, stone, mud, purling snow,
Grimace—

IX

Out my window near the Missisquoi,
I stare at squirrels, flitting nuthatches.
I have a view, in the cold winter light, of yellow birches.
I hear them snapping—cold sharp sound, and I turn my head
From a rude lawn of snow,
From the hemlock, weed stubble, the iced-over river,
To that canvas on the wall. And she is, how shall I say it,
There—unfinished—unfaced, impossible

To portray. And if truth is to strike away
What lies, what obstructs, what brags and brays on,
My eyes do it if my hands are quiet,
Playing with a cigarette, not much else,—
The eyes know what they should've known before—
The eyes know that stroke after stroke is to be
Unstroked, undone, truth then this—the unstroked
Surface, and she in all her untrifled
Unseeable splendour, not some poor art.
But then, if better art, it's poor love.
For what's art, really, but love, love of a
Thing, and of the pains required to make it
So—love of a thing, of a being, she—
But I'm tired, I'm ruined, being open-eyed,
And I set water to boil for my tea.

X
And a sacred kettle whistles like a kiss
That would announce its glad-heart presence.
There's nothing like love that knows its laws,
And I'm momentarily—oh dear—uplifted.
It's as when, the other day, old, old Egypt getting new—
Boiled over—went and threw its tyrant out
And the world was exposed for its shabby
Conduct, all the world that loved a bully
For a hundred reasons or more, maybe
None. And this is forever: truth only
Breathes for an instant, then it's broken down—

XI
There she is in the shack's half-light, she so ancient and of the moment,
Half-painted because half-imagined, half-seen, as it were,
Her eyes wandered too close together, that lip

More of a curl than it ever was,
That bosom too self-consciously proud
(She was not 'fetching' if no prude),
The waist, the arms about right,
And further down, yes, that's—well—her,
And those narrow, delicate feet such as betrayed
Her inherent power, the rage I missed in her look,
For if she only knicked her man she killed Jim Light,
And yet I breathe and mull my attack,
The complementary colours, the tempering ones
(That green under the blushing Cezanne fruit)—
And the whites, yellows, blues, the applications of which,
Who knows, might make for familiar flesh.
Can I cause them to cohere
If she was no more than a shallow bitch?
Or if she was my Beatrice, my soul's way out?

XII

And so I could, I think. I could flick a switch
And flood the shack with the appropriate light,
And see a canvas, discern shapes on it—
Or a geometry of limbs
Or a psychology of eyes
As when she'd wound and lust and trick herself, that way,
Into redemption, back to her so-called marriage.
So yes, the question goes without an answer still:
Who was she with me—who was she with him?
Did her boredom pinch them off, the passions flying around,
And render answers beside the point?

XIII

And I could cheat and forget the face,
The full frontal, and merely paint

How she'd turn herself sideways, that lilt of her shoulder
When she most wished to score her debating points
And her hair would seem to billow down,—
Or how she'd cause a third eye to form, forefinger pressed to thumb,
Just before she'd lie to me, saying yes, she was sweet on Jim Light
So would he stop being such a bore about love?

XIV

The winter light of an afternoon angles,
Sweeps and withdraws, akin
To something made of silk
Hushed across the snow—something made of silk
Raising goose-bumps on the flesh.
I sit by the window, cigarette lit.
Logs in the airtight crackle with heat.
Good moment. It's one of those moments
Of a pleasant delusion—as it all makes sense,
The hundred reasons why Jim Light can't build her face
Because only half-seen, half-imagined untruth
Due to an excess of desire that was once truth,
The only one, pure necessity (even if we never had need of it),
Which is the hell of it, you know, the crazy thing,—
So he must give 'Ida' up or paint his reasons,
Paint his own so as to paint her deadly demons
In a proper time and space, the world uncertain—

§

Tacitus in the Afternoon

—The treatment Tacitus the historian accorded Tiberius Caesar has always raised eyebrows

I

That writer of history taking the shade
In the peristyle with his shrubs and blooms,
Reflecting on the nature of truth,
Is quick to the paradox of truth
That is every unspoken heart,
Caesar crucial to his pessimistic views.

For live long enough, you'll come to know,
When it comes to that which cornered you,
You only betrayed yourself
Far worse than friend or foe
Managed to direct your bent.

The absolute silence in the laughter you hear,
In the humming of an insect, in the sun's wide rays
That break on the surface of the ornamental pool—
All of it confounds your inquiries
Into why a certain class of fool
Behaves as it does, those Caesars—

II

That writer of history taking the shade
Forgets himself: he grabs his head,
Not from pain so much as wonder.

And it's elbows down on the elegant
Ebony table, the curved legs of which terminate

In a goat's nimble feet, all the better with which to dance
On that most absurd ground, tragedy.

And though that past is antiquity, he's near,
As near as the corner of your eye and mine,
Our conversion of value to parody
Almost complete. The historian reasons:

*"It's seldom acknowledged that the brighter stars
Of a political firmament, high on acclaim, are dupes
Of their bright features. Wanting love, they bring to love
Circuses of hate. And for me here taking the shade
In the peristyle with my shrubs and blooms,
There's Caesar's reign of terror to outlast
With pleasure in life intact."*

III

The bleak fellow that you see there in the shade,
He with his shrubs and blooms, with his dark hyacinths,
Is thinking a dark thought even as
He's using all the dark thoughts up:

That the mute fishes in their pool,
As they flash about in their element,
Catching light on their scales, seemingly without care,
Might as well have been the senate
That, losing its way, degenerated—
Band of brothers turned flunkeys.

For Caesar allowed the best and brightest
To gather, to debate, to doublethink
Their ritual applications of conscience.

"Oh yes, a man might solve much,
And, in solving, accomplish little."

IV

The sun just now is a kind of laughter,
The way it plays about on surfaces,
On water and marble and bronze,
On olives glistening with oil,
On a dull gold coin of Caesar,—

On the mind that would seek self-understanding
But labours in the dark. Wasn't it as simple as this—
That when there were fortunes to be made, when life was good,
If pointless, then living it up was the best life of all?

Yet live long enough and sanctuaries fail.
The moral thing to do? Alleviate pain!
Still, moral feeling gets beaten down
Even in the best men of conscience.
Busy moralists never seem to learn
That silence, sometimes, speaks loudest
And most tellingly when, comics tittering,
All there is is noise—

V

But what truly possessed one, what impinged upon
The bougainvillea in the corner of one's eye,
The brooding, piss-washed stones of empire,
That intricate chorus of swallows in the sky,
Was the comradely grin of desire.

Prayer? Why pray, the gods giving you their backsides?
High on its worst instincts, the world runs

Proudly supreme, runs roughshod a while
Over those benignly asleep, who hurt no one, who maim all,—
Over the wishful dreamers blind to the writing
On the wall, for whom there's always time
To shop for the best judgment and best justice,
Who intend great things and set loose chaos
In hearts and minds.

How pretty those wild flowers in their pretty beds.
How sharp the thyme and savory and else,
All of it an exercise in building memory,
The heat building of an afternoon—

VI

The man you see there taking the shade,
He will mumble aloud to a dead Caesar,
To Tiberius, that is, to the grim, dour one
Who saw only the worst in the human mind
As he was intimate with his own.

The man you see there of an afternoon
Taking his holy shade in proximity to
Diana the goddess whom he adores (as he used to hunt and loves her
woodlands),
Went hard on the record of Tiberius Caesar
Who secured what Augustus brought about
Or the peace after the wars.

VII

What loosed in Tiberius was willed blindness,
A predilection, it's said, for sexual encounters,
Those cherubs in his villa's pool, *that this defined him*
As he leered at death and understood

That, try as he might, he might've done more
To right some wrongs, everyone up to no good—

And the ant you see there with its articulate legs
Going the rounds of the flower pot –
It tells us what might've been
Had we not made government.
And the bird with its eye on a crumb
And the fishes of a fountain-splashed pool—

VIII
But the silver-haired historian, eyes welling with impulse,
Though the situation is pretty, the air pungent with herbs,
With the warm caresses of a breeze
(Diana the huntress all marble and shade)

Scratching out words on sedge, bitter words for the thing
That has his every loyalty, knows how the poisons of politics
Invite life's poisons,—

And even Caesar can't deny the abyss,
Can't say his share has been lovely and precious,—
Can't always arrange things to advantage,

Unlike the ant going around the pot,
Unlike the bird with its rational eye,
Unlike the silent fishes over whom
Massive cumulus passes.

—Tacitus: Pliny is always sending me his verses,
          weaselling for compliments—

—Tiberius: Poetry? Pah. But it's harmless enough—

IX

Then, as if preordained: America!
The colonial, scrappy, boisterous business,
And now here's conviction, here's the slap-happy passion,
Now here's the thing once again made new,
And we are the idea and the excuse,
The antagonisms in us nothing more
Than so many degrees of difficulty—

X

So that we are divided even now
In the only places where we cohere,
And all the disparate pieces drifting in us
Pine one for the other and look
For the ceremony that will join them.

§

Open G for Blind Joe Death

In a California coffeehouse
You struck the strings of a big guitar.
Finger rolls and slides and strums,
Judgment Day in the whisky jar,
Love and falling out of love.
And now your music comes around again,
Your marches, your waltzes—time's cotillion.
You in your grave, I hear you once more
In the lacunae, the lacrimae,
In all the spent dreams of life.
You'd been far-seeing with your
Finger-picking style—

—John Fahey, of all the exponents of your instrument
America in her blisses and agonies spawned,
The most Arcadian, the most caustic of them,
You orchestrated for our delectation
An American Dis in seventh chords,
You Mississippi John Hurt and Theocritus,
Blind Blake, Bukka, Patton and Virgil
Of the Eclogues messianic and otherwise,
Your years, what else? bittersweet:
1939–2001.

About the Author

Norm Sibum has been writing and publishing poetry for over thirty years. Born in Oberammergau in 1947, he grew up in Germany, Alaska, Utah, and Washington before moving to Vancouver in 1968. He founded the *Vancouver Review* in 1989 and has published several volumes of poetry in Canada and England. Sibum currently lives in Montreal, Quebec.

Acknowledgements

The "Sub Divo" section of this book was previously presented as a chapbook, printed by Biblioasis, with a cover image by Mary Harman, 2011.

"Open G for Blind Joe Death" appeared in *The Bow-Wow Shop* at some point in recent memory.

§

This book is dedicated to various Stalwarts, some of whom have been attentive readers of the preceding verses, and have had the odd thing to say for or against them.